Aaron's Crossing

Aaron's Crossing

A True Ghost Story

by

Linda Alice Dewey

NORTHERN SPIRIT BOOKS

Empire, Michigan

NORTHERN SPIRIT BOOKS
Published by
Northern Spirit Creative Productions, LLC
7627 South Dune Highway
Empire, MI 49630

www.lindaalicedewey.com

Author's Note

*This book is a work of creative nonfiction. The events involving the author actually
took place. The other events may have. The author of this book does not advise ghost-
hunting or ghost-busting. Attempts at connecting with the spirit-world without the
guidance of an experienced* physical *teacher (often available through metaphysical
bookstores) is unadvisable. The intent of the author is only to offer information that
may help you on your own path through life toward spiritual and emotional well-
being. Should you use any of the information in this book for yourself, which is your
constitutional right, the author and publisher assume no responsibility for your
actions. Some names have been changed to protect the living.
Aaron's middle and last name have been changed to protect his family.*

❖　　　❖　　　❖

Publishers Cataloguing-in-Publication Data
Dewey, Linda Alice
    Aaron's crossing : a true ghost story/Linda Alice Dewey—Empire, MI:
Northern Spirit Books, 2005.
    p. ; cm.
    ISBN: 0-9767193-0-4
    1. Burke, Aaron. 2. Channeling (Spiritualism) 3. Spirit writings. 4. Ghosts.
    5. Parapsychology. I. Title.
    BF1473.B874 D49 2005
    133.9/3—dc22   0506

Cover design and graphics by Todd Bauerle
www.toddlbauerle.com

Printed in the U.S.A. on recycled paper

For Mom and Dad

PROLOGUE
Michigan, 1995

"Someone's here. The hair on the back of my neck is standing up," Lisbeth whispered.

I felt a dense heaviness in the air. Someone we couldn't see belonged here. If the gravestones gave any indication, he lived at least a century ago.

We separated and wandered the soft path, reading the markers—some easy to decipher—others, mottled with the dark gray of dead mold, were more of a challenge. The little graveyard deep in the woods appeared to be abandoned long ago. Headstones tipped at odd angles, and a rusty wire gate swung into oblivion.

Lisbeth stopped in front of a space with no headstone, dropped to one knee and crossed herself, forehead to chest, left side to right—appropriate if she were Catholic. But Lisbeth was Jewish. To this day she doesn't remember doing it.

"Why did you do that?" I asked.

She looked at me, her eyes large black flowerheads, her voice husky. "I had to."

My brother, who had brought us here, feigned reading a brass plaque while he watched us from a distance.

"Do you feel anything?" I asked him.

He rolled his eyes. "I don't feel a thing." The truth is that this evening would spook him for years to come.

In the forest, night falls early and it would be even darker on the path back to the van. I felt such longing to reach out to this poor being, whoever he was, but could do nothing except say a prayer before I left. As we walked along the path back to the car, I looked back at the abandoned burial ground—dormant, still, alone—its secret hidden by the forest. How awful to be stuck in such a place.

Over the next few years I returned twice, the first time with my family in the middle of the day. The sun shone, but the place still felt eerie. This time I brought my camera. I'd heard that ghosts sometimes show up on film, but when I got home, the camera was empty. I'd forgotten to put film in it.

On my third visit I couldn't stand it any longer. *He was there*. I could feel him, sad and helpless. I *had* to let him know someone cared. But what could I say that would be meaningful to a hundred-year-old ghost—something so universal it would sail across the time-gap between our cultures so he'd understand?

It came to me from out of nowhere, and in that moment, the wheels of an impending miracle began to turn.

"Whoever is here," I called out to the emptiness, "my heart is with you."

And nothing would ever be the same.

Now the woods felt even spookier. I turned to see my friends disappear down the path. "Wait up, you guys!" I yelled. No one slowed down. They wanted to get out of there, too.

As I hurried I wondered, *Could he think my call was an invitation?*

Was he following us? It did feel strange behind me. *No,* I told myself. *I'm overreacting.*

I caught up with the others. Feeling silly and carried away by my imagination, I said, "That was corny."

"What was?" my friend Carolyn shot back.

"What I just said. What does it mean, 'my heart is with you'?"

"It means you care."

"Yes, I care."

As we drove away, I checked the back seat. "What if he followed us and he's in here?" I asked.

My son, Evan, spoke up. "He can't be in here. There's no room."

But the ghost did follow us out of the cemetery, though I didn't know for sure until he physically broke through the next day. Any doubt I ever had about the existence of ghosts and an Afterlife vanished when I saw what he did.

I thought I might be able to help him. This book is the story of what happened.

❖   ❖   ❖

Years after our journey together, I wanted to know why he became a ghost in the first place. What was the Afterlife really like? Did I hear him accurately when we communicated? I wanted to write about it but needed more information.

One morning, half-awake but still in bed, I heard a male voice in my head.

"Aaron! Aaron! Wake up boy. You're comin' after me."

He pronounced the name in a way I had never heard: "ah-RONE," with a roll on the "R." I didn't understand the command,

"You're comin' after me." I thought he must have meant, "You're coming with me." But I knew who it was and what it was.

I hurried to the computer and began to type. As I listened, at first I only heard single words. Then, a phrase at a time. I typed what I heard, never knowing what would come next or where it was heading. When I finished that morning, I had five pages, beginning the story of Aaron's life. Months later I would have a full, though rough, manuscript.

I often feel ghosts now. Rare is the graveyard that does not harbor at least one mournful soul. But I do not venture in to find them, for they may not be so benign as Aaron. This one time though, I didn't stay away. I was foolish and fearless, and I'm glad I was, just that once.

And so I give you Aaron, telling his story in his own voice, just as I heard him in my little cottage in northern Michigan.

PART I

I

DEAD
Ohio, 1922

For a moment, I didn't feel a thing. I opened my eyes and looked up to see the other farmhands gaping down at me.

"His neck's broke!"

"Yep."

"He's dead!"

"Looks like it."

I got up and brushed myself off. "I'm all right," I said, but they ignored me. "Look, I'm fine," I reassured them, but they stared at the ground. I looked, too.

At first, I didn't realize it was me—the head twisted at a forty-five degree angle, eyes wide open and mouth ready to cry out. But the clothes were mine, and I shaved each day with the help of a reflecting glass, so I knew what I looked like.

With horror, I lowered my gaze to the arms and legs and trunk I stood in now, separate from the body on the ground, yet still intact. I didn't understand.

Another hand ran up. "He dead, Bill?"

"Yep."

How could I be dead when I still existed?

"I'm not dead," I said to them. "Look!" I thrust out my arms and waved them around.

"What do we do?" asked Jake.

"Gotta take him into town, I guess," said Bill. "Call the boss."

Jake ran off toward the farmhouse.

Crusty hadn't said a word till now. He looked at the grotesque body on the ground. "Wasn't my fault. I loaded the hay up like always. Wind must've made that bale swing like it did."

"Aw, they all swing, Crusty," said Bill.

"Yeah? Then how'd he miss it?"

"Wasn't looking, I reckon."

Truth was, I hadn't been looking. A mouse scurrying along the loft's floor ran over my shoe. Kicked at it I did, reaching for the bale rope at the same moment. Lost my balance is all I can figure.

Killed because of a mouse?

The hands stood around as Boss Delvecchio approached, then explained what happened as he bent to listen to my heart and feel for signs of life.

"He's dead."

"That's what we said."

Dead. There is my body lying in front of me, but here is my body I'm standing in.

I stood directly in front of the boss. "Look at me, for God's sake! I'm okay."

"Better hitch the wagon and take him to the undertaker," Boss said, obviously not to me.

Kneeling, I touched the body on the ground. It felt like sponge. The slightest pressure and my hand sank into it yet re-mained visible, an unpleasant pressure all around it. Wrenching my hand out, I searched the face, ugly and grotesque. Repulsed, I pulled away and moved off as they brought the wagon around and loaded it up.

As the horses began to move, I hopped into the back and rode along. I looked beside me at the distorted remains again, then down at myself. I had no use for the loathsome carnage next to me. Wasn't me any longer, that I could see. The body I was in suited me now as well as that one had before. Felt a little lighter, actually—no aches or pains, although I must say I felt tired. *It would be natural to feel tired going through all this*, I told myself.

Boss and the help deposited my remains at the rear of the funeral home. Bodies are always delivered at the rear in an effort to protect clients from the more unsavory aspects of the process. Boss went around to the front—where the living enter—and into the office, where the real business takes place.

The undertaker, a Mr. Murphy I believe his name was, asked many questions. "Last name?"

"Burke," said Boss.

"First?"

"Aaron."

"Middle?"

A pause. "Don't think he had one," mumbled Boss.

Murphy looked up. "Didn't have one, or you don't *know* if he had one?"

"Don't know," admitted Boss.

"Mr. Delvecchio, with all due respect, we need complete death records. Once we fill out this certificate, it gets filed with the county. Having complete information is most important."

Boss nodded. Now, may I say that one of the best things about working at this particular farm had been his lack of curiosity about his workers' past. I hadn't even filled out an application. For all Boss knew, I had given him a fake name. He hadn't cared at the time. But he was in trouble now.

I hadn't wanted anyone snooping into my past, finding out I had left my children and all. Nothing wrong in what I'd done; I just didn't want to talk about it. Made me uncomfortable.

Murphy continued asking questions, but Boss didn't know anything—date and place of birth, mother's maiden name. Nothing. The undertaker put down his pencil and looked at him. "You do know how he died, don't you?"

Boss described it fully.

"You were there and saw it happen?"

"Well, no," he admitted, then brightened, "but three of my hands did!"

Murphy nodded, then said, "I don't suppose you know about next of kin."

"No."

"Well, Mr. Delvecchio, whom do we notify?"

Boss was silent. I had worked at his farm for the past four summers and had never once been asked about my family.

Murphy sat forward, leaning his forearms on the desk. "What shall we do with the body, with no one to notify and make decisions?"

Boss looked down at the hat in his hand. I had never liked Boss, but I liked the working conditions on his farm. He didn't bother me, and I didn't bother him. But I didn't trust him, either. Now I knew why. He did what befitted him with no thought for anyone else.

"We can store it for a day," said Mr. Murphy, "but after that, we bury."

Boss nodded.

"You'll have to put the word out. Advertise. If no family comes forward, it'll have to be the community cemetery with a small service. Do you know his religious preference?"

"He never went to church that I know of," said Boss, finally able to say something true about me, "but he's Irish, so there's a fifty/fifty chance he's Catholic!"

"Catholic it is, then." He made a final note and slapped the book shut. "Next, will you be taking care of payment, Mr. Delvecchio?"

I thought Boss should pay, since I was on the job when I died. He had other ideas though, and I knew right then that he'd take the money from my personal effects. I didn't know what he would do with the rest—a sizable sum it was, too, me working all those years with few expenses. But he would make me pay for my own funeral, that was for sure.

"I'm good for it."

Upon hearing that, Mr. Murphy slowed up a bit. "Ah, it is possible, Mr. Delvecchio," he ventured, smiling for the first time, "to raise the quality of the proceedings. Perhaps a nice hardwood casket? Or a visitation this evening?"

Boss would have none of that, and they concluded business.

I felt torn at this point as to what to do. Should I follow Boss back to the farm and see what he did with my possessions, or stay and see what Mr. Murphy did with the body? Both belonged to me in life, after all. More attached to the body, I decided to stay.

Murphy opened a ledger and continued to write after Boss left. Soon, a rather officious man who must have been the coroner blew through the swinging doors from the front of the funeral parlor. "Lyle," he said, tipping his hat to the undertaker. Taking a form down from a shelf, he asked, "What do we have?"

"Fellows from Delvecchio's farm say he fell from the hayloft." He rose from behind his desk and led the way to the back of the building through another set of swinging doors and into a room lined with shelves. My dirty, ugly corpse lay on one of two immense marble tables in the room's center.

"Cause of death," the visitor glanced at the body, "broken neck." He signed the document, left a carbon behind and walked out the door.

Murphy approached the cadaver. "Broke your neck, did you, you old fool?" he said when the door closed, speaking directly to my body. "Couldn't keep your head on straight, could you?" He chuckled to himself.

I didn't laugh. Neither did my corpse.

Since there would be no family to see me, he wasted no time bathing or cleaning up the body, but slung it into a pine box without ceremony, pushing my limbs so they'd fit. The way he treated it appalled me. "Serves you right for ogling girls the way you did."

I never ogled any girls. Stayed away from all of them.

"Turning your neck this way and that. Got carried away, didn't you?" He laughed aloud at his joke. "So many pretty ones to see. Pretty soon, your neck can't take any more." He laughed even harder.

The man was beginning to irritate me.

"Then you see one that really knocks your socks off, try to get a good look and break your neck!" He shut the lid on the casket and walked off, roaring. "Damned women'll get you one way or another." His voice faded as he passed through the swinging doors.

Angry, I picked up a pencil and threw it at the doors. He poked his head back in, saw the pencil roll on the floor and picked it up. Sobered, he set it on the counter, looked on every side of the room one last time, and left.

Knew I was there, didn't he?

I strode over to pick up the pencil, but this time my fingers passed right through it. *Now, why,* I wondered, *could I do it a moment ago but can't now?*

Tired. So tired was I after the events of this day. I needed to rest. Deciding the table was better than the floor, I lay down and wondered how I could be on it without falling through it. I rolled onto my side and passed my hand back and forth through the table. Now I was really tired and closed my eyes.

Dead, I thought. *I'm dead.*

❖   ❖   ❖

When I came to, the rising sun told me it was morning. I hadn't actually slept, but the rest helped, and I felt more energized.

Mr. Murphy entered in black undertaker's regalia. Horse and hearse waited outside. He and another man loaded my casket. Once again, I rode beside my corpse.

We were on our way to my funeral, but was I really dead? When people died, they stopped existing. At least, that's what I had always believed.

Which brought me to the thought of my dear Susanna and how I mourned at her grave, believing her body lay beneath. And Katy before her. And Mrs. Harris. And Mummy. I had thought them all dead and gone. But what if they were around like I was now?

The thought of Susanna being here excited me. Why shouldn't she be? She had to be somewhere, didn't she? If I existed after death, wouldn't she? Wouldn't everyone? I guessed we did. After the funeral, I would search for her. And then I would find Mrs. Harris and Mummy and Katy. Happy thoughts these, after all this shock and confusion, and I concluded the ride in a more cheerful state than I had been since Susanna's death.

Before I knew it, the undertaker and his helper opened the back doors and unloaded the casket. I jumped out.

The grave already dug, the gravediggers waited a distance away, itching to get on with their work. A few people stood at the burial site—boss and a priest in black, and some hired hands in work clothes, for they would return to the tasks they had left. That was it. A pitiful showing, especially since none of them really cared about me. They'd shown up out of a sense of duty. At least there was that.

The priest made a few remarks. Since he didn't know me, he couldn't say much about me personally. None of them really knew me, for that matter. "He was a good worker," was about as far as they could go. "Never bothered anyone," was another good one. The priest concluded with the Twenty-Third Psalm and the "ashes to ashes" verse, then made the sign of the cross and blessed it all in the name of the Father, the Son and the Holy Ghost.

Ah, now *there* was a word. It occurred to me for the first time that I might just be what was known as a ghost, and not a holy one, either. If I were a ghost, what would that mean? That Susanna and my mother were not here after all? Were there even such things as ghosts? If so, were others here? Did everyone become ghosts or only a lucky few? How long did we stay this way? Forever?

As the group near my grave dispersed, I looked around the place. I had noticed—without really thinking about it—a few other people at nearby graves, some standing, most sitting. I had thought them to be mourners, but now I could see that these were not like the others. They seemed lighter, not as dense as those leaving my grave and the gravediggers over there.

These people had gone through death! Don't ask me how I knew, I just did. It was as if a second subtle layer of existence covered the mortal realm. I didn't think of them as dead, since they still existed, just no longer in the Physical Layer.

I began to explore, looking at one grave, then another. There were certainly more gravestones here than their visitors, which meant that everyone wasn't here. Where were the rest?

Seeking answers, I approached a woman seated in front of a grave. "Excuse me," I said.

She didn't move.

"Hello?"

She looked up slowly, and I beheld a fatigue beyond anything imaginable.

Turning away, I moved on. "Morning," I said to a man lying on his stomach by a grave up the hill.

"Morning," he mumbled into his arm. He rolled onto his back and looked up at me. "You're the new one, then." He looked tired, too.

Come to think of it, I felt tired again. "May I sit here?" I looked at the headstone. "Esther Fielding, 1849-1900." Not his grave at all.

"My wife."

I nodded. "Where is she?"

"Right here, you numbskull!"

I walked on. A young woman sat with her ankles crossed on a grave over by the cemetery gate.

I tried again. "Morning."

"Good morning," she said, smiling. She patted the earth next to her. "Have a seat."

I obliged, grateful for someone to talk with.

"New, ain't ya?"

I nodded.

"What happened?"

"What do you mean?"

"How did you die?"

"I fell."

"Oh." She chewed on something. Funny, I hadn't thought about food since the fall yesterday.

"I fell, too. Horse fall."

"Oh." Then, "That's too bad."

"Nah, it was good."

How could it be good?

"Got me outta there. I hated working."

"What type of work did you do?" I asked, more to keep the conversation going than out of real interest.

"I was a Lady of the Evening."

"A what?"

"You know. A prostitute."

Until that moment, I hadn't even thought of her as a woman. Uneasy, I began to rise.

"Don't leave," she said. "I'm not a whore now."

I relaxed and sat back down. "No, I don't s'pose you are."

We sat for a while as the sun moved west at a pace I could watch. Amazing how quickly the time passed.

I indicated the unattended graves. "Where are all the others?"

"They went."

"Went where?"

"Anybody still here usually leaves after a while."

"Still here?"

"Anyone that doesn't cross." She looked at me. "You don't know nothing, do you?"

I shook my head. "Not about being dead."

"When you die, they come and get you—most of the time. Sometimes they don't."

"Oh." Then, after a while, "Why not?"

"Now if I knew all the answers, would I still be here?" she asked, annoyed. "Look, if they didn't come and get you, they didn't come and get you!"

I got up and walked off to see what they had done with my grave. Filled in, it was, a mound of dirt covering the top. I had missed seeing the last of the box, but then, it wasn't me in there anyway.

Twilight had descended, so I decided to lay on this plot of land belonging to my "body" and camp for the night.

I could get more answers tomorrow.

❖   ❖   ❖

Before I knew it, the sun was high in the sky again. My neighbors were in the same spots as yesterday. One old man leaned against a tombstone. I walked over to him with the hope of learning more about existence in this Second Layer.

"Morning," I said.

"Well," he grunted, "at least you didn't say 'good'."

"Didn't say 'good'?"

He raised his voice. "Didn't say, 'Good morning.'" He looked up at the sky. "'What's so good about it?' I would have asked.

Nothing good about anything, far as I can see." He shifted his back against the gravestone, scratching it back and forth.

"You been here long?"

"A while." He sat silent a moment. "Saw them bring you in yesterday."

I nodded.

"Pathetic small showing, I will say."

"Well, I'm not from here."

He squinted up at me. "Then why are you buried here?"

"They didn't know where else to send me."

"Ah, now that's a problem, isn't it? And you too dumb to tell them."

"No, I never told them."

He leaned toward me, "And you didn't tell them afterward either, I'll wager." It had been a question. He waited for the answer.

"I was dead. How could I have told them?"

"There are ways, there are ways." He leaned back again.

I sat down.

"Watch it!" he yelled.

I jumped up.

"This is my plot. *Mine!* And I won't be sharing the only thing I own on earth with some stupid sonofabitch who doesn't know his ass from his hole in the ground, and doesn't care enough about the living he left behind to let them know where he is."

"Wait a minute," I said, equally angry. This man had judged me when he didn't even know me. "I was dead. How could I let them know?"

"Oh, for God's sake," he said, exasperated. "If you're desperate enough, you'll find a way." He turned away.

I walked back to my grave and sat down. *If I were desperate enough*. When I'd been angry, I could throw that pencil. Maybe there *was* a way to let them know where I was after all!

Now I had to ask myself if I *wanted* them know I was dead. Maudie would be sad, for sure, but what about the children? Would they miss me? Or would they be angry with me? They couldn't really think I'd abandoned them, could they? Didn't I leave them in good care, and the house with all that money in it? True, I never communicated with them again, but I had been wretched over their mother. Maudie knew how they reminded me of Susanna. She would have told them.

I supposed they did have a right to know what happened. After all, I was their father. And I owed it to Uncle Sean and Aunt Louise. And Kathleen. And the O'Connors. And Maudie, of course. I really should let them know I was dead, shouldn't I?

But how? The old man said if you were desperate enough, you could do it. Was I?

I was tired, that's what I was. Not desperate at all. Laying back, I closed my eyes. I had to recuperate from the trauma I'd been through, that's all there was to it.

❖   ❖   ❖

When I opened my eyes, night had fallen. Whether it was warm or not, I couldn't tell. I couldn't feel temperature. The wind blew locks of hair across my face, but I really didn't feel the wind itself. I did feel my hair move, though. Strange. I could feel the texture of the grass, but again, not its temperature.

I had not been hungry nor thirsty since dying. Neither had I felt ill in any way. There was no pain in my neck, and my joints didn't hurt like they had when I had been living. My body did seem a bit peculiar. I could move my arms and legs and such, and feel things on the outside, but I didn't feel my insides.

In fact, if I were dead, I wouldn't need to do certain things like eating to keep me alive, would I? And I wouldn't be susceptible to disease, either. So was I immortal? Could I be killed?

"Well, you got part of it right, anyway." The whore was at my side. "You ain't gonna die again." She sat down and lit a cigar.

I watched as she smoked it, wondering how it all worked.

"Easy," she answered. She knew what I was thinking! "Just takes a little energy, is all." She blew rings into the air.

"May I try?"

"Sure." She handed the cigar over, but it fell through my fingers onto the grass. She sighed, picking it up. "I *said,* it takes energy. GOD!" She jumped up. "I *hate* having to repeat myself." Throwing her cigar into a stream that ran through the place, she trounced back to her plot.

What was wrong with *her?* Come to think of it, everyone I'd met here so far had some kind of weird attitude. It never occurred to me that I fit right in. I just knew these people were unpleasant, and I wanted to move on.

Gathering myself up, I dusted off my pants and marched through the cemetery gates. Middle of the night it was with no one around. I walked about town, looking into store windows, hiking the few residential streets, investigating. Dogs barked as I went by. At least *they* knew I was there. I cogitated upon this as I walked out of town toward the farm. A mile later, exhausted again, I sat under a tree by the side of the road and closed my eyes.

Next thing, it was morning again. I hadn't slept, just closed my eyes, and when I opened them, time had passed!

"It's staying in their time that does it." The whore had found me. "If you don't do nothing but sit, time passes real fast. But if you take part in anything worldly, it slows you down and takes your energy. That's why you see so many of us just sitting around, doing nothing."

"But what about when you and I talk to each other?"

"It's easier, because we're on the same level, know what I mean?" She tilted her head to see if I was getting it.

I nodded, "But when we walk, we're not using anything from the Physical Layer."

"But we're moving in their space, see. It's kinda hard to understand. As long as you stay still, you don't get as tired. Course, it's boring as hell."

I wanted to ask something else but didn't want to intrude. I decided to ask anyway. "How long. . ." I began.

She finished my question. "How long have I been here?" She shook her head. "Too long. Course, time is different for the living. But in their years, I've been dead a good fifty or so."

I sat back. Fifty years!

"Oh, that's nothing. Some have been dead more than a hundred, and that old lady you first bumped into, the one that could hardly roll over? She's been dead more than two hundred. Least that's what the others tell me."

"How'd she get that way?"

"Longer you're here, the less energy you have, is my guess; but I don't know for sure."

Like getting old. The longer you exist, the less vital you become. Time takes its toll no matter which state you're in.

Yesterday. . ." I began.

"Yeah, I was a little curt. Didn't mean to be. It's just so damn frustrating the way most folks get taken across except for people like you and me." She sighed. "It isn't fair, and I don't get it."

"What do you mean, people are 'taken across,' and 'they come and get you'?"

"You watch. Get near when someone dies and see what happens. Won't be like what happened to you and me, I'll guarantee you that. When they come," her eyes became dreamy, "the sky opens, and some sorta pathway appears for them to walk on. All kinds of people are waiting to welcome the new one to the Other Side. I've even seen them hugging and kissing just before things close up."

"Close up?"

She looked at me, cross again. "You know how I just told you the sky opens up?"

I nodded.

"Well, then, it *closes* up!" she looked away. "God!" She stood. "I can't take this. I'm going back."

I got up and proceeded toward the farm. It wasn't long before I became tired, but a wagon came by so I jumped in the back, enjoying the ride. It, too, took a toll on me, and I realized I was participating in their time again.

"Takes it outta you no matter what you do." She was beside me again.

I looked at her, surprised. "How did you get here?"

She rolled her eyes. "You got a lot to learn."

I looked at the driver, but she shook her head. "He can't hear us." Then paused. "Most of the living can't, anyway."

"*Most* can't? You mean some can?" Hazy fragments of childhood stories about the fey—seers from the Old Country—surfaced in my memory. But more confusing was how she got here.

"You can do that?" I asked. "Just go from one place to another?"

She laughed.

Now I was the one getting irritated.

"Hey, I can't answer two questions at once. I'll take the second one about moving around from place to place.

"Think about it. Our time isn't as slow as theirs, so why should our space be like theirs, either?" The expression on her face said she was making perfect sense, but I didn't understand. "Our time goes faster, so that means we get to places faster than they do. Oh, you can do stuff at their speed if you want, but that'll just take it out of you."

I must have looked confused.

"Look," she said. "Haven't you noticed how thick the living look? Like they're really heavy?"

I nodded.

"We're lighter than they are. Lighter than air, really. All I have to do is think really hard, and my body lifts up. Then I think of the place I want to go, and I'm there!" She smiled. "Now, that's real Trans-Portation." She laughed at her joke.

"You flew here?"

She nodded.

"So I don't have to ride to the farm? I can fly there?"

"Only if you know exactly where you're going. Doesn't work all the time." She closed her eyes, lifted out of the wagon and was gone.

If we were more ephemeral than the living, it *would* be easier to transport that way!

She was back. "It's all thought anyway," she said and was gone again.

She could transport herself anywhere simply by thinking of

the place. And she could read my mind. I remembered how I knew right off that Boss Delvecchio would make me pay for my own funeral. It's not like I heard his thoughts, just knew his intention—could feel it. It was all thought. You did it in your thinking, and your body responded. I was going to try it.

I sat in the wagon, closed my eyes and relaxed for the first time I could remember. Hadn't felt this way in years, light as a feather. What else was there to do but go with it? My body lifted slightly off the wagon. Opening my eyes, I stayed up. I willed myself higher, then forward. A propelling action in my mind, like focusing in the direction of a sound barely heard, moved me ahead. I pushed my attention forward with all my might and moved. Quickly. Letting up some, I slowed to a manageable speed then slowed down completely and brought myself to a gentle landing by the side of the road a quarter of a mile in front of the wagon.

I felt marvelous, no longer heavy and drained, but light and bright and ready for anything! This was amazing! So many limitations lifted away! I could go anywhere and wouldn't be seen. Spectacular!

No one could bother me anymore, aside from the occasional being from this Second Layer, and I could visit the living at any time without being disturbed by them. Ever since Susanna's death, I had just wanted to be left alone. Now I had my wish.

I began to laugh. I laughed and laughed and laughed at the beauty of it. "Just leave me alone," I had said over and over again. Oh, not to their faces—except once. But in my head I wished they would all just go away. Now they could bother me no more! It was the answer to a prayer.

Then I sobered.

Except—except for the times I was with Susanna or Mrs. Harris. My loved ones—I didn't mind having them around. Even Maudie. Kindhearted old Maudie. She had done so much for me. They all had. I sat and thought for a long time about all the things those good people had done for me. I wondered what I had ever done for them. I couldn't think of a blessed thing. Why had they been so good to me?

Aunt Louise had taken me in when she didn't even know me, just because I was family . . . and Susanna—I had done for her what any lad smitten with such beauty would have. But I was never overly generous. Well, I did buy her that sailboat. In fact, for a time, there was nothing I wouldn't have done for her. But how much had I done unselfishly for those who mattered to me?

Did I really ever love anyone?

2

KIDNAPPED
Ireland, 1891

"Aaron! Aaron, wake up, boy. You're comin' after me." My father's harsh whisper woke me. He rustled the blankets, pushing them back, finding my wee body all warm and cozy and settled in for the night. In a swoop, he had me quick in his arms and out the door.

"Aaron, now, there you be lad, with your daddy, like a good boy. There, there now." He slung me over his shoulder like a sack of potatoes, wrapped in my comforter. Rushing down the street we went, as I glimpsed the stars through a crack in the covers.

I remember thinking, *Where's Mummy?* I didn't hear her. Couldn't see her, for sure; but I didn't hear her, either. I couldn't hear my brothers or sisters, but that didn't mean anything. We had all gotten our bottoms spanked too many times to disobey him. If he had told them to be quiet, I didn't know. But now I couldn't hear any noise other than my father's footfall. Maybe they were behind a bit. Or ahead. Maybe that was it.

I whimpered.

"Shhhh!" Sharp was his voice, tainted with such an ill will as made me suddenly awake and afraid. Now I was in my *own* head, alert and afraid. There were *no* other foot noises. He was taking me somewhere without them and wanted me to be quiet.

I whimpered again, thinking, *Father, where is Mummy?*

"Hush!"

It was all I could do not to cry out, but then he might take the belt to my backside. I didn't want to be bad. I just wanted Mummy.

Tears wet the coverlet now. Back then, I always cried. The smallest of the band, I was wee little Aaron, running around getting into mischief one minute, hiding behind Mummy's dress the next. Hid me many a time, did Mummy from Father. Didn't like his wrath any more than the lot of us, and suffered the brunt of it for our exercises. She was a good one, was Mummy. We saw her take it for us time and again and never a peep out of her.

Cold now. I felt it creep in through the comforter. He had me over his shoulder still, looking like a bag for sleeping or something other than what was in it, for I was very small then. Four, I believe I was, when he took me away.

My tears did me no good, and I let myself drop, relax and fall into a drowse—not easy to do with all the jostling. His steps rapid and deliberate, we went and went until I thought he could not mean to go more, and still we went farther and farther away from home, away from the family, away from Mummy. Each time I awoke, we were farther away, and the tears—how they ran down me till the comforter was soaked, and I was cold, cold, cold all the way through.

After a long time, the first light glimmered inside the covers. I shivered mightily, and still we went on. My father didn't stop until the sun was fully up. Then, I felt him make a swift turn and walk through some high grass. Breathing heavily, he stopped and threw me off his shoulder, laying me down somewhat easy, yet still hard for a little boy.

"There, now. There's a good boy. Open your eyes, Aaron. 'Tis only I, your daddy, with you."

I opened my eyes to see where he had brought me.

We were nowhere. A thicket entwined us so I couldn't see farther than his shoes on his feet stretched out in front of me. How he got into it, I could not figure.

I looked at him lying by my side—tired, out of breath and covered with sweat, although it was not warm out. His coat, his good coat, was torn at the shoulder and below the elbow. Mummy would have to fix it.

Mummy. "Where's Mummy?" This I needed to know before anything about eating, which was my next question.

"Hush, now. Let's sleep a bit. Then we'll talk." All my life, if my father said to do something, even in his Nice Voice—which he used now—we all did it then and there. So I settled into my comforter, miraculously finding dry spots, and went fast to sleep.

❖   ❖   ❖

We slept through the day and by nightfall were out and moving again, much the same as the first night except that we got going sooner and, that being the case, some traffic passed us at first. When he heard a wagon, he moved off the road, stumbling around until he found a good place to hide, for hiding he was doing. Then we were out again, traveling down the road at a smart clip.

I soon came to understand that we were indeed going far away, and that Mummy and the others were left behind. Sad, it made me, so sad. To be with my father only and not have the love and comfort of Mummy to protect me was a rotten thing. But I was a wee one and could go inside to my own magic world and devise things there that no one could take away. So there I went.

Since we slept most of the day, I was awake at night now, which made the trip more difficult. I could stay withdrawn for only a while, especially if I needed to relieve myself, which little boys do more often than their parents. This made for problems, since my father had it in his mind to make headway at all costs. Mind you, I did warn him before I let it all go the first time, and he hushed me much the same way he did that first night—not in his Nice Voice, but in his real one, his mean one. However, once nature took its course a few times and we were both soaked through, he came to respect that one need of mine like he never respected anything about me before nor since. If I needed to go after that, we stopped, no matter how far we still had on our journey.

When we paused for food, it was always at night. Scroungers now, we learned that the best places to look for scraps were behind the inns and saloons, for they threw the lot of their goods out before going home. We filled my father's coat with food for the coming day, and off we went, thieves in the night. We were never hungry.

It seems that we traveled this way for several days, but I cannot fully reconnect to that time, the entire event confused me so. I filled my thoughts with those I loved and wondered what would become of me. I had no idea where we were going.

On the third evening, I began to hear noises all the time—cats meowing, dogs barking in the distance, horses' hooves clomping along the street. I recognized it for a street now and not a road, for I heard their hooves on the cobbles. We must have been in a large town, for the sounds to continue so long.

After a length of time my father slowed, then turned. We went on for another bit, and then he slowed and turned again. He turned so often, I thought we must be going in a large circle, but in a while he slowed for the last time, then stopped, put me down on my feet and unwrapped me.

What a sight! Middle of the night it was, the moon hung suspended high in the sky. The town was all aglow. Lampposts threw pools of light onto the ground everywhere. Why? I could not say, for nary a soul lurked about. Yet in the distance I could still hear the occasional horse and rider, the infrequent wagon, the intermittent bark of a dog. So some were about but not right where we stood. I heard other noises, too—strange, unfamiliar sounds I did not recognize.

In front of me a gathering of buildings such as I had never seen continued on and on without stop as far as the eye could see. Not pretty new buildings like you saw in our town, but old, rundown and so much bigger—some four floors high! Most were of brick or stone, others were of wood. All had signs telling who worked inside.

After filling my eyes on this spectacle, I turned around for another surprise. A road led to a wharf filled with ships of all sizes and kinds—cause enough for a boy like me to gaze in wonder. But dwarfing them all loomed a great big steamship! Huge, in fact. I had never seen a ship of any kind, but there she was, a queen amongst the others, alive before our very eyes, exhaling moonlit puffs of steam out of a pipe at her crown. People bustled back and forth below, loading and unloading cargo like little bugs crawling up the arm of a giant beast.

This ship was the biggest thing I had ever seen. Barring the good Lord's, its power was greater than any around, and I puzzled why she breathed but did not move when my father spoke to me for the first time since setting me on my feet.

"Well, Aaron," he said, "this be our home for the duration of our journey." I looked up at him. He gazed at the ship. So that huge boat would take us wherever we were going? Where would we stay? The only place where I could see people on the boat was way up on top. The thought of being inside it (which, I found out after finally asking, was where we were to be) filled me with terror. And the first time she blew her horn, I thought I'd be blown over. No one could be heard—their mouths moved, but no sound came out. The ship's horn covered all.

After standing and gawking, my father led me toward her. Frightening it was, to be so close to it. As we walked nearer, its sides swelled out, blocking our view of the top. The ship moved ever so slightly, just a sway now and then to let you know it sat in water, which scared me all the more, for it was not stable as I had thought when viewed from afar. More like the little boats I played with on the pond at home. A ship on the sea is still a boat on water, for all that.

Home. How far away and different it seemed. Already dimming in my mind, I could hardly conjure it up in the face of this mighty monster whose very presence muted all memories, taking them from me then and there. I would often be in a mood later in life to muse and think on the place of my earliest childhood, but I could never bring it fully into my head after seeing this ship. It was as if I were no longer in the same world, and without the strength to hold onto what I couldn't see while beholding this, I let go of what wasn't and went with what was.

3

At Sea

The Atlantic Ocean, 1891

By midmorning, the wharf teemed with people of all kinds. The men had never stopped loading and unloading. Cranes lifted heavy items on board.

People who did not appear to be workers began arriving for the ship, many ferried in lovely carriages and dressed finer than I had ever before seen. They looked neither right nor left, but straight ahead as they walked. The uniformed man checking tickets at the bottom of the ramp called them by their last names, smiling grandly. They did not say much in return.

These people did not have much to do with those unlike them, I thought, for they were barely polite and didn't give workers such as the ticketmaster the time of day. I was young, but observant, and could see things already.

There were also people like my father and me. Dressed more comfortably than those arriving by carriage (though not many with a torn coat like my father's), the adults spoke with passengers and workmen alike, while their children chattered and danced around, laughing and playing tag just like we did at home. The grownups didn't talk much with the children except to give orders or admonish them.

I, however, did not share the excitement of the other children, but felt lonely and abandoned even with my father next to me.

He knew a man he thought could get us on the ship. We had been told to wait while this friend worked a deal for tickets with someone on board. The friend did not return for a long time, and I feared he had forgotten us when all of a sudden there he was, right in front of us.

We stood, then my father reached into his long coat and took out his father's solid gold watch and handed it over. I'll never understand why he did that, as there were other things in the house of equal value. We had not been wealthy, but we did inherit a piece or two of finery along the way. All of us had been taught that these pieces were sacred. None were to ever go out of the family for any reason, so why my father passed over this watch which had been so dear to him is beyond me. But there you have it, and I'll not bother about it again except to say that this voyage must have been dearer to him than anything in the world.

Which left me to wonder why he was taking *me* along. He never did things with me, like playing games or even helping me build a toy. He took no interest in my business—not like I did in his—so I could not fathom why he wanted me with him. He didn't want me for company, so there was no flattery in it. Perhaps, I reasoned when I was older, he knew that as I grew, I could help him work in our new homeland. Then, too, people might not ask questions of a man with a boy along. It would be good cover for an escape. But at the age of four, it was a mystery and a troubling one.

My father took the tickets, the men shook hands, I grabbed my comforter, and away we flew. He had me by the hand and nearly pulled me off my feet, so fast did he walk. Wanted to get aboard before anyone found out or changed his mind, but I couldn't know that, and I ran alongside as we approached the ticketmaster.

This man, who smiled so at the more grand, barely gave us a look, and I could see he was just like the finer-dressed sort—he didn't really care about the heart or soul of a person, just his money. I knew that then, just as I know it now. You can judge a person by how kind he is to the poor—if you can judge a person at all, that is.

I hadn't known we were poor, just that we dressed different-ly. I thought it was our choice to be the way we were. That some-one could be "outclassed" by another was silly. A person's mone-tary value could not determine his worth as a human being. I have found since my passing that this sort of person suffers a great deal on the Other Side for their lack of humanity.

We moved up the ramp behind the others, showing our tick-ets once again at the top to an officer who pointed the direction for us to go, down the hall to the left and then down a steep stair-well. At each landing, we turned and went down again. Never hav-ing been inside anything except a cottage or church, entering this massive hulk was like being swallowed up. I wanted to see what it looked like going in the opposite direction until we looked out from that high place I had seen from outside. But at the rate we were going down, I didn't think we would be topside often. It did-n't bother me that we would not see those finely dressed people, but I so wanted to see the water and watch the men work.

Reaching bottom, we landed in the biggest room I ever saw. It stretched in all directions, unfurnished except for lots of long tables fixed to the floor in the center of the area with stools alongside. People settled in at its perimeter, hanging blankets or whatever they had for privacy around the spaces they were to call their own.

My father eyed the expanse, chose the direction he wished to move in, and move he did with me in tow to a corner away from everyone else. I looked at children chatting with their mummies and daddies and could not help but wish we were a family, my daddy and I.

He hung up my comforter to mark our space, emptied his pockets of the less valuable items and sat down on the floor with me beside him. I looked up and wondered if my comforter would come down for me to sleep with or if it would be there for the duration.

Hours later, though the noise in the room had mounted to the level of cacophony, a rumbling underscoring the hubbub suddenly swelled. Gently, I felt the slightest movement, and my father spoke for the first time since we boarded.

"Now we're away. They won't be starting the engines full throttle till the tugs have pulled us out to sea. Then you'll hear them!"

Had he actually spoken to me? Amazed, I looked up at him, waiting for more, but none came.

We sat for what seemed many an hour. I entertained myself by watching others, a pastime I still enjoy. It was interesting to figure their ways from what they did.

I could see that for some, building the nest was most important. This would be basically the women with families, even if it were just a husband. (I figured that any woman accompanying a man would be a mother or daughter. I was not aware of illicit relationships until later in life when it would affect me greatly.) For others, developing friendships and camaraderie with neighbors took first priority. They talked and laughed in groups made up of women or men or children, but not mixed company.

Those like us with nary a smile nor a word to share—the lone ones—watched others or looked at some book brought along for the voyage. Many wrote remembrances on a scrap of paper, though the poor light made either of these last two undertakings difficult and many could not read or write. Some set up housekeeping, but most, like my father and I, had what they brought on their backs and not much else.

Suddenly, an enormous hunger came on me from seeing our neighbors eating crackers. I looked at my father sitting still as ever and wondered if he had any food stored in his longcoat. He still wore it, for it was cool belowship. I was cold, too. I looked up at my comforter. It would have helped.

I also had to go again, and when I finally gathered the courage to tell him, my father rose, then looked back down at our space. After spreading our few things out a bit more with his toe to mark it, we began a search for the loo. He walked around but finally had to break down and ask. A woman pointed to an area over in the corner with stalls. That was the place.

We went to stand in line. Before the trip was finished, the entire lower quarters would reek the way that corner did, but at this point only a small area stank, and I was glad we chose our living site early for I wouldn't want to be staying over here.

My turn now, I entered the stall, pulled the door to, and faced a slop pot with a larger can next to it. I did what I had to, then slopped it into the bigger, partially filled can. Outside, a basin and pitcher with plenty of water waited with a tub next to it. My father filled the sink, and we each washed thoroughly. Returning, we found our space as we had left it, for no one wanted a fight at the beginning of the journey, and fight my father would. Those around us knew it by the looks of him.

He was a rough sort, was Edward Burke. Many a late night he came home roaring drunk and had it out with my mother. Sometimes, as I peeked through the slats of the loft, I saw him stagger about, blustering and betting that she hadn't done this or that while he was gone. Then he went to their bed and gave her Holy Hell. I knew that term from my brothers. They said he gave her Holy Hell, which was usually followed by his falling across the bed half-clothed and passing out. Mummy slept on the floor by the fire for the rest of the night.

I wondered what he must have been like earlier on those evenings. Usually, he went to the tavern, but sometimes it was to a neighbor's for a draught. Was he mean with his drinking friends, or did he just save it for the ones who knew what he really was? My father thought himself passable at hiding his roughest side, but the layer of wellness he wore on his exterior was thin indeed, the rest there to see if you wished. I myself learned to wear a thin mask of heartiness some thirty years later, but I couldn't understand it then, and I can't really say I understand it now.

At any rate, the other passengers respected our space, and that was good enough for us. In a while, the engines increased their loud thrumming, and mates brought down trays loaded with pitchers of beer and platters of meat and potatoes and bread. We were to supply our own plates and utensils, of which my father and I had none.

"Go ask," he said, indicating the family next to us. The mother passed out tin plates to her husband and at least six children. She stood for a moment, a few plates still blessedly in her hands. How they could afford this trip with such a big family I'll never know, but there they were with things to spare, and here we were with only the shirts on our backs.

I walked the few feet over as she began to put the extras away. "Excuse me," I said in my most polite voice. She continued rummaging through her gunnysack. "Excuse me," I repeated, louder this time, then tapped her on the back.

Whirling around, she almost hit me with the plates. "Oh sonny, I'm sorry. I didn't hear you." She smiled at me with her eyes first, then asked, "Did you need something?"

I eyed the plates. She looked across at my father who gazed in the opposite direction as if unaware of the chore he had sent me on. Looking back, the woman saw where my eye fell.

"Have you no plates then?"

I shook my head.

She handed me two. "Bowls?"

I shook my head again.

Rifling through the sack, she came up with two. "Cups, utensils?" The woman didn't miss a thing.

After that, Mrs. Gunnery supplied whatever we needed, and the whole family took me under their wing. "Papa" Gunnery (he insisted I call him that from the outset) called me "Sonny," making me feel a part of the crew. He played the Irish flute while the children danced, then set it down to pick one or two up and twirl them around as he whistled the tune. "Come on, Sonny," he'd say, and I'd hop up and run over to their space where the fun was. So many times he'd surprise us with a paper bird he'd make, or crawl around growling like a bear, making the girls scream and Mrs. Gunnery shake her head, hands on her hips, laughing—a jolly man if ever I saw one.

When I looked back at my own father, he'd look away, ignoring our play. Did he feel left out or that we were improper? Did he care at all? I couldn't tell, and he wouldn't say; so I played, and we settled into a routine.

It turned out that "steerage" passengers (that would be us) could go topside often, and we took full advantage of the opportunity to breathe the fresh sea air after being in the monster's bowels.

"Can you wait till we get there?" asked Buddy, the youngest Gunnery, as we roamed the deck our first full day out to sea.

"Well," I began. How could I admit that I didn't know where we were headed? I took the direct approach. "I'm not sure where it is we're going."

"Why," said Buddy, "we're off to America, that's where!"

America!

Happy was I to be going to a place so many had dreamed of. I only wished Mummy and the others were with us. Mean of him not to include them.

I later came to suspect that he ran away with me because he had gotten himself into trouble back home. Perhaps his irate ways at night created an irreversible situation, and he saw this as his only escape. That particular scenario I believed to my dying day, and I can now say that I wasn't far off, discovering on this side that he did indeed murder a man that night—someone he angered in the pub. They had taken it outside where the deed was done. I do not know the details except to say that my father wronged the man, then silenced him.

There are many things we think we will never know. Life is a mystery, and one muddles through as best as possible until the end comes and the sense of it all is revealed. But what I pieced together as a child was as wise as the piecing I have done since. Children, you see, are more in touch with their inner reality than their teachers and life trainers, responding to the outside from the inside, until the adults around them force them to reverse the process, removing this glorious awareness of what is.

The days became weeks and passed quickly until one blustery night when the lights went out due to a storm. Down below, we rolled and pitched. The children cried, and everyone became ill with the movement, except for my father. Mrs. Gunnery had all of her family to care for as well Mr. Gunnery, who was more ill than most. She did not look too shipshape herself, and little need did she have for a rummy like me to beleaguer her further. So I in my misery, cared for myself. Laying on my side, I used our borrowed bowl when I could hold it in no longer.

My father never responded to my need. For a child of four this was difficult, and after that particular evening, I never asked for his help with anything to his dying day. It would do nothing but anger him to be pulled out of his reverie, and whenever I needed help that badly, the last thing I wanted to arouse was his anger.

Eventually the lights came on, the ship stopped its exaggerated rocking, we began to feel better, and things returned to what we had come to think of as normal. Aside from Mr. Gunnery, who continued to worsen.

"Oh, Papa," Mrs. Gunnery said the day the sea became calm, "are you not better?" She looked closely at his sallow, moist face, taking his hot hands in hers. "Papa, you weren't well even before the seas turned ugly, were you?" He closed his eyes and moaned. "Methinks this is more than the seasickness," she said.

Now, the ship's doctor only came below when someone had already died. Those around me guessed the passengers upstairs paid a fee for the doctor's services. The truth is that the ship was understaffed, with only one doctor assigned to the vessel, thus fulfilling regulations but putting the lower paying steerage passengers at greater risk.

Poor Mr. Gunnery died one week later. The doctor came downstairs to pronounce him dead, and Papa was taken away for immediate burial at sea. The danger of contagion on board was extraordinary. Some already complained of symptoms similar to his, voicing a well-found fear that the illness might spread. We all went above for a brief ceremony, then down he slid off the board and into the ocean.

Our lovely woman next door was besieged with grief. Unable to console herself, much less her children, she now faced life in a new country with eight mouths to feed besides her own and no husband. The immense lot this woman carried on her shoulders showed itself in her bearing and on her face but most of all in her manner with others. No longer the smiling, helpful neighbor you could count on, overnight she turned into a dour, sour old lady you avoided at all costs.

Angry she became when her children laughed or messed around with other children, for she did not want trouble and yearned for simplicity. So they weren't allowed to play with others like myself. Instead, they passed the time after chores playing with each other or in some silent pursuit like practicing their letters or drawing on a slate. If they did not, they were not allowed to go above the next day, a fate almost worse than death to all of us below the water level.

Looking around, I saw that the other children had already made friends and were even quite tight with some. I would be on the outside of those friendships. After sitting by my father for a few days, I became fidgety and decided to find things to do on my own. At length, I began quietly exiting his grasp for short periods, gradually extending these forays to hours at a time. Realizing he did not care if I wandered, I was soon off on new adventures for the whole day.

Soon, I found the crew's quarters and hid under a table to spy.

An old sailor pulled me out by my shirt. "Look what I found!" he exclaimed.

"Well, well, well," said the cook. "A street urchin, if ever I saw one. What's your name, boyo?"

I couldn't speak, so frightened was I, for surely they would take me back to my father.

"He don't have a name," said another. "Let's call him 'Mascot'!"

They adopted me as Mascot, and I began to warm to them, showing up in the strangest places. They'd whoop when they discovered me, and it became a game. They laughed at anything I said. If I answered their questions sincerely, they laughed at my seriousness. If I quipped, they laughed even harder. Often, they showed me an instrument or something out on the sea, telling fictitious stories just to get my reaction, my widening eyes of shock or surprise sending them into gales of laughter.

Never having captured the attention of an adult other than Mummy, I became heady with the thrill of being noticed. Soon I was dancing for them. They threw pennies, and my feet flew. Sang for them, too, any ballad or rhyme I could think of. They laughed and laughed as they swilled their ale, and I worked to keep them happy.

Once, I wasn't at my father's side for a whole night. Instead, I slept on a rookie steward's cot, one who had been sent home after being indisposed to the sea his first day aboard. The lack of space inside the quarters had been his complaint, and I now believe the man was claustrophobic, although at the time they didn't know about such things. The other crewmen laughed at his plight, making sport of his absence throughout the trip.

I craved my time with the crew. They took me in and showed me things and fed me foods I had never dreamed of. It was a lively time, this, rewarding me an hundredfold, for here I found I was worthy. I did not realize that these sailors, having been out to sea for weeks now, were starved for entertainment, and I provided just the diversion.

When they would go about their business, I went about mine. Good at staying out of the way—for hadn't I learned to do just that at home when my father was in a rage?—I watched what everyone did. Things went on in each of them that they thought no one saw. It came up on their faces or in their gait or posture. These sailors weren't as happy as they would have others believe. As do so many, most wore a happy mask disguising a pain that ate away at their insides.

I have always had a knack for seeing what people were made of. Perhaps it came from watching my father, The Chameleon, first one side of him showing, then another. Perhaps from watching my mother struggle, or my sisters and brothers ranking themselves in superiority according to age or ability or some other silly thing important to them at the time. Whatever the reason, I had the knack by the age of four. The peculiarity of it was that at times, it seemed I knew things about people they themselves were unaware of. Usually, I kept this to myself, as it was frowned upon for a little boy to speak of what he knew to an elder, especially if he disagreed with what the elder espoused. Later in life, it would cause me to avoid others, for the things I saw were often unpleasant.

For now though, it served to pass the time and further dull my memory of the Old World.

4

BOSTON TO CHICAGO
Boston, 1891

They brought the boat to dock at a busy wharf in Boston. I knew it was Boston, for all on-board talked of it—whose people were here, how plenty of space was here for those like us, how children like me waited on the docks for their rellies from Ireland.

Happy was I to see land as the next bloke. These last weeks at sea had not been easy. I, for one, was as worn out from the strife below decks as from that what brewed between the crew above. The only entertainment around to be had, the sailors discarded me as land drew near, and I found my way back to my father's side without a word from him as to my whereabouts.

He and I forged ahead with the disembarking crowd toward the deafening hubbub at the dock and felt our feet touch solid earth once again. People sang and laughed and cried, were serious and worried or frivolous and bedeviled by the new land. The ones on dock shouted over each other looking for loved ones, while others tried to grab our attention with items we might need for the next portion of our journey. Men representing companies from many areas of the country needing workers stood collecting audiences of immigrants like us.

It was not a very welcoming new land, what with the treatment we got at customs. We stood in long lines for hours only to be told to go to other lines. But the time finally did come when we were on our own in the New World. Of course, no one called it the New World anymore. That was from times past. But it was a New World to us. And a New Life—a time of establishing just what we would do in this new land and how we would do it.

My father expected me to be his shadow—go where he went and do what he did, but silently so as not to be noticed. And so I sat at his feet wherever we went that day and the next and took refuge within myself, receding farther and farther into a world full of idiosyncrasies and imaginations that were never a bore.

First, as I have mentioned, I entertained myself by observing the ways of others. Or I ignored all around me and delved into my own remembrances, already so blurred that I sometimes wondered if they had ever been real at all.

But I missed Mummy. I felt it in my bones, in my head and worst of all, in my heart. A physical ache I felt not only for myself but also for her. I had been her favorite, don't you know. Knew it from the softness in her eyes I did not see when she looked at the others. Maybe it was just that I was the youngest, but I don't think so. There was a connection, an attachment that went beyond flesh and blood, beyond mother and child, into realms one does not see with the eye nor hear with the ear. I could feel her still and knew she could still feel me. Each of us feared for the other, for neither was safe and secure any longer.

I would hear many years later that my mother died of a broken heart, for she had lost the one she loved most in the world—and it is not my father I speak of, thank you.

So there I would go in my head to what I could remember of this woman. Talked to her I did, and she answered, sending such loving feelings that I felt all warm and cuddly inside, sitting at his heel, oblivious to all but my mother and me.

Once through customs, all sorts of doters accosted us, wishing we'd listen to their *spiel* as they stood on their soapboxes appealing to our "better sense." But my father had a plan of his own, and we set out right away for Dorchester Street, wherever that was. Turns out we had a cousin there, one Jeremy Burke, son of my father's eldest brother, said to have made great inroads in Boston with his business. After much asking about for directions, we found ourselves away to the south of the wharves and back farther into town—all of this on foot of course, for my father had not a farthing to offer for a ride to this place.

At last we came to 710 Dorchester Street. What a disappointment! Ramshackle at best, it was old and not made of brick and stone as were the houses of Ireland I had known, but of wood that even covered the broken windows. The neighboring dwellings were not much better and it became apparent Cousin Jeremy was not as well off as he would have his cousins back home believe.

I doubt my father had a backup plan, so he knocked on the door with no response. He knocked harder, which was useless, for it was a small place to begin with.

A neighbor across the way heard the knocking and peered out the door. He stuck his head back in but not soon enough, for my father saw the movement and quickly hurried over to query him. After three good knocks on this door, the neighbor opened it a portion. An old eye, a nose and two fingers were all I could see.

"You'll not find what you want there," he said when my father asked of Cousin Jeremy's whereabouts. "Gone for work he is and lucky to be having it, if you know what I means," said this one. An odor wafted through the crack in the door, and I did not want him to open it any farther.

"When does he get back?" asked my father.

"Not till dark, it won't be. Not till after dark, most probably. They has to work when they cans, you know."

"We'll just have to wait, then," said my father, and we proceeded back to Cousin Jeremy's step where we sat ourselves down for the afternoon. I fell asleep after a while, but it seemed not long before my father shook me.

"Here he comes, boy. Look sharp!"

I awoke to look up into the face of one it seemed I knew from as far back as I could go. This was the face of Ireland on the visage of our cousin, whom I never had met, yet knew without reason or doubt.

"What a small lad to be making such a long voyage on that big ship!" he said. Tall, lean of build, and not too old—certainly not yet thirty—he laughed as I looked wide-eyed into his twinkling eyes. His clothes, soiled with the day's work, were tattered and unmended by a woman's hand. He held his hat in his hand, exposing hair dirty and tousled, for hadn't he worked hard all day? And his teeth carried the stain of smoke. But it was the eyes that held me, for the light had not yet gone out of them, a light that carried itself back through the ages—the light of the survivor in us.

"Ah, Cousin Jeremy, and good it is to see you, boy," said my father in his most gregarious voice. The user in him came into its prime when he sensed someone had the means to help him out. He no doubt could see that Cousin Jeremy was not the kind to leave rellies out in the cold and would do whatever he could to help us out.

Indeed, the younger man unlocked his door and welcomed us in, overjoyed that kin right off the boat would visit him with news from Ireland. The interior of his place held up to the promise of the exterior, furnished with table and chair, a stove and little else besides the pallet he slept on. We brought in our blankets and few belongings, piling them in the corner. I had slept on the floor before and could do likewise here.

A pot of tea brewing, Jeremy pulled up two crates for sitting and plied us with questions of Ireland, home and family. My father and he kept up a bantering conversation full of laughter and warmth. You would not have known my father, so full of social graces and goodwill from abroad was he, telling tall tales of the doings of people I had lived with up until a month or so ago. Utter stories they were, weavings round the truth for the teller to share with the wistful listener. I watched my father with some admiration for the talent he showed, recalling days long ago when he told similar tales around our table at home. My father, The Story Teller, shone in the lamplight as he strewed about this or that tidbit of the loved ones Jeremy had left behind.

You see, Jeremy had jumped on ship, working his way across the Atlantic at the young age of seventeen. Having seen the famine and pestilence of Ireland, he believed better could be found elsewhere, following his dreams to this new land. When it was time for Jeremy to tell his story on this evening of evenings, it was not quite the same as his letters back home. Yet in a way it was, for the truth shining in Jeremy's eyes said that he had not yet let up dreaming of better things, even from this hovel of a house he lived in at the moment.

Jeremy told of a place far west of Boston with work for all—a town much newer with everything clean and ready for the workers needed to man this kingdom. "Everyone's talking of a place called Chicago," he said as the night wore on. "Sits on a freshwater coast that goes for hundreds of miles. All the fishing and swimming and pure drinking water you'd ever want." In rivers, creeks and streams the fresh water flowed, needing neither to be boiled or brewed—water as fresh as could be had in the world right there in your own front yard. "They're building out there fast as they can and hire all who come along. For good wages, too!"

"Where did you say this place is?"

"Oh, it's way Out West, at least a thousand miles. You'd have to take the train to get there."

"Sounds good. I like that it's away from the more populated seacoast." My father didn't want Boston relatives breathing down his neck is what he meant.

Jeremy had the gleam in his eye for this place. "Ah, Edward," he said, leaning forward, "I envy your ability to go where you want. If I weren't so tied down to this place..."

"What do you mean, tied down? What's tying you?"

"Well," said Jeremy, looking at the room, "I got myself in a bind with this house."

"Sell it! Rent it! My God, man, if you're wanting to go, don't let that keep you. You only live once, you know."

It hadn't occurred to Jeremy to rent the place; but the gleam was there and the dreamer took over. Next morning he visited a realtor and on his way home bought provisions for the trip. The following afternoon saw us at the station acquiring tickets, which actually turned out to be the winnings of a wager.

My father was nothing if not a bettor, his poker face one of the best I have ever seen. That was one of the reasons he could never be trusted. No matter how he acted, you couldn't be sure that some trick wasn't up his sleeve to take you for all you were worth—and didn't he do that to me time and again!

He won this bet at the railroad station. I know not the issue it was over, but right away we were off on a train. Jeremy, full of excitement and optimism, regaled us with stories of Chicago. He told of lovely salons and fine restaurants, of easy jobs with big paychecks and lots of women. This last was an aside to my father who had lent a mysterious air to the disappearance—not of ourselves from the Irish countryside—but of my mother instead.

The stories my father told were as full of life on the downside as Jeremy's were on the upside, and I could no longer tell fact from fiction. I wanted Jeremy's stories to be true as much as I wanted my father's to be false. Yet I could not assuage the doubt that welled inside as I listened to my father's sad tale. But what I thought of it mattered naught to my father. I was baggage to him, pure and simple.

But I wasn't baggage to Jeremy! He unlocked within me a place fast becoming unknown, and just in the nick of time, don't you know. I feel that, had I gone without someone like Jeremy or Mrs. Gunnery on that trip, I would have locked myself up, forever unable to communicate with another soul. For many years to come, I would be fortunate enough to have someone I could relate to. However, there would come a time when not a soul would be able to console my heart, and I would become truly lost.

But I am ahead of myself and must get back on track. I rather clung to Cousin Jeremy during the train trip, and for good reason. Not only did his winning presence draw me; he unwittingly became a protector against my father's sour temper and meanness. As Jeremy and I fooled around, giggling and laughing, Father began to see that I could be put to use, given the right situation. So use me he did as I innocently cozied further up to our cousin.

The train ride grew long and full of stops for people to get on and off. Jeremy lent me his window seat, and I watched tree-covered hills submit to high mountains. Then unfolded a sweet land of milk and honey with flowers and foliage the likes of which I had never seen—especially the trees. I was not familiar with wooded land, and I liked it, though at times it became rather dark and scary.

Evenings, we stayed in our seats, though others had berths for sleeping. My father and I had learned to sleep anywhere, but Jeremy squirmed throughout the night. Sometimes, rustled by his restlessness, I opened a sleepy eye to see him looking out at the black night, dreaming no doubt of opportunities coming round the bend.

At last the conductor said we must get off at a busy station in Chicago itself. I couldn't see any water at first, though they said it was just "over there." And yes, if I looked to the east, I did see several ships lined up and the blue water beyond.

Hailing the nearest taxi—actually a flat-bottomed wagon pulled by a dray—my father and I climbed in back, Jeremy up front giving the address to the driver. Starting up, we did not know how long it would take to get to this place so we stayed alert, expectant always to jump down. After a while, however, we relaxed and watched others going by attending their business.

These people seemed happier than those back in Boston. They walked with purpose and seemed to know what they were about. Plus, we had not been accosted at the station as we had been at the wharf by those looking to get our money.

The latter, of course, was nonexistent, though I do believe Jeremy had a little something, for weren't we riding on a carriage he hired himself? Aye, my father had a way of getting what he needed by hook or crook. Would that I had the same talent, but it wasn't in me to connive.

Presently, we found ourselves in a newer area of the city. The houses, small and rather pushed together, featured yards out front and space enough out back so a boy like me could play and be seen from inside the house. Children abounded here, their mothers in back hanging up clothes or pushing baby carriages down the street.

At our destination, Father and I grabbed our blankets and few belongings, while Jeremy paid the driver a nice fee, his smile fading for a brief moment when he heard the amount. My father looked down and away, not wanting to be part of it.

Before we got to the front door, a couple of mongrel terriers accosted us—happy barkers—accompanied by screams of delight from a woman coming 'round the sideyard.

"Jerry! Jerry! God in Heaven, is it you?"

Jeremy picked her up and twirled her around for all the neighbors to see. "The apple of me eye you are, Neecie, there's no two ways about it. So let's have a look." He put her down and stepped back with an appraising eye, its twinkle barely hidden as he looked her up and down.

Now my father, mind you, was not blind then nor would he ever be when confronted with a beauty. He stood not a hair's breadth from me, saying nothing as he watched these undertakings.

But "Neecie," short for Denise, had married Jeremy's best friend just before they moved to Chicago the year prior. My father's interest waned as quickly as it had waxed when he learned of Mr. Divine. Bored with Neecie, he inquired about Johnny's work and Chicago in general with the greatest curiosity. He was on again, off again, tiring of keeping up a front around Jeremy. The strain began to wear the edges of his temperament as he looked about the place, restless, waiting for Johnny to come home. I braced myself, but his temper never crossed the line to real irritation.

Neecie and "Jerry"—for that is what they called him—lost themselves in the telling of their sagas, the one to the other, all afternoon. Johnny had won a foremanship, then a superintendent's position building houses not far from here with a team of Irish workers from the area. They were still hiring, for plenty of houses awaited building.

After tea, I relaxed and laid down as the chatter and laughter droned on. Neecie had been nice to me, mind you, but clearly her mind was on Jeremy, for her eyes shone as his had when he saw us that first time. Now he was the one with news from loved ones back home.

I fell asleep, but soon Johnny turned up the walk.

Neecie ran out, screaming at the top of her lungs, "Johnny! Guess what? Jerry's here!"

Dropped his lunch bucket he did and ran to kiss her, then swung open the screen door, his presence filling the room with health and happiness. Though the light behind him dimmed, the glow from the lamps within shone on a being larger than life itself. "Jerry! I can't believe my eyes! 'Tis too good to be true! How is it you're here, man? Whatever brought you away from that pesthole of a place you call home?" He moved back from the hug that enveloped both men. "And look at you!" he laughed. "Scrawny as a chicken and just as good-looking."

"Ah, 'tis a story I have to tell you, Johnny. And it is so good to see you. But first, I have some kin I'd like to introduce, if you don't mind."

Johnny turned around in surprise to see my father and me.

"Johnny Divine meet my cousin, Edward Burke," Jeremy said with a flourishing gesture.

Johnny stepped over and engaged my father in an energetic handshake. "And pleased I am to meet you, Mr. Burke."

"Pleasure's mine, I'm sure," Father said with all the warmth and gusto as he could muster.

Johnny swooped down to my level. "And who do we have here, may I ask?"

"Why, that's my cousin Aaron," laughed Jeremy as Johnny picked me up.

"And a fine specimen he is indeed," said Johnny. "How old are you, boy?"

I'd swallowed my tongue deep in my throat as he lifted me high above his head. Never had I seen such a big man, hence, never had I been lifted higher. Having always thought my father big, Jeremy was at least a head taller, and *this* man was a giant in my estimation. My father had instructed me that he would do the talking for us, and I've since ascertained that he didn't want me to say anything that might reek of less than the goodness of his care. It didn't matter now. I couldn't talk anyway.

"He'd be four, if I'm counting right," my father said.

"Only four years old? And where would it be you come from, if I may be so bold?"

"They got off the boat late last week and came to see me," offered Jeremy. "They'll be looking for a place to live with work, don't you know. I suggested they come this way, and before you knew it they had me coming with them."

Johnny put me down, then turned to Jeremy. "And Jerry, will you be staying, or are you just visiting? For glad I am to see you, there's no two ways about that. But if you're wanting work, I'll have to get about finding just the right kind, you know."

"Ah, Johnny, any work will do for now. You know that." He laid a hand on Jeremy's shoulder.

"Aye, and I also know you to be a master craftsman, not satisfied with less of the job nor less from yourself." He looked from one of us to another. "All right then, so be it. Jobs are aplenty here, that's for sure."

He turned to my father. "And what type of work would you be looking for, Mr. Burke? I might be able to help you, too. Many friends we have made in the time we've been here, haven't we, Neecie?" he asked his wife with a smile.

My father laughed, attempting to be as gregarious as the other two. Not too good at it anyway, his laugh was false. "I'd be pleased with any work not strictly indoors."

"Building then? What skills do you have?" Johnny asked as we moved to the dining room where Neecie had supper on the table.

"He's good with animals, being from the countryside and all," suggested Jeremy.

Johnny spoke of a neighbor up the street, a Mr. McGregor, who was constantly at him to work for him in the animal pens at the slaughterhouses. "You being familiar with animals, I could get you in with him right away, methinks. They're crying for workmen down there in the worst way."

Now, my father had worked with animals all his life, but good with them he wasn't. He looked upon them as things without feelings, not beings at all, and believed they were there solely for the use of humans. This job would suit him grandly, I am sorry to say, for he would be taking them to butchery. I sat next to him, sipping my soup, knowing this even at the age of four.

The conversation at the table centered around the types of work available, Chicago's booming economy, the situation as it stood in Boston when Jeremy left, the whereabouts of old friends and neighbors. Then they agreed to go down to the corner pub after dinner for a brew. Old Mr. McGregor would surely come 'round. He always did in the evening, don't you know.

Worn out, I slipped from the table and crept a second time to the corner, rolling into my comforter for the first good sleep I'd had since the night my father took me from my bed, my mother, and the only home I'd ever known.

5

GOING TO WORK
Chicago, 1891

My father and I lived in the first-floor flat of a two-story home not far from Jeremy, who took a room at a boarding house around the corner. Johnny and Neecie lived another street over.

Father worked at the stockyards, raising himself before dawn, though the summer light came early and stayed late. "You have to be there before the cattle rouse or all hell breaks loose," he would say. So off he went with nary a word, as I would still be fast asleep.

When I awoke, I would shuffle to the icebox. A crust of bread and milk, and I was doing well. Often, beer and something from the night before lurked in its dark cabinet. As I hadn't yet developed a taste for the brew, I would pour myself water from the 'stern, take whatever was there to munch on, straighten my clothing and be on my way.

All sorts of children played outside. It looked like such fun, I couldn't wait to join in. But I was shy and said naught for nearly a week, till they wondered if I wasn't a dumb one. I'd been right to stay quiet though, because when I finally did say something they laughed and pointed at me.

"What'd you say?" asked one boy.

"I said, what is it you're doing?"

He and the others laughed and laughed. *"What is it yer doin'?"* they mimicked.

Different than the kind laugh of the sailors, their ridicule twisted my insides. I ran and hid in the shrubs at Jeremy's until he came home after work.

His eye caught my movement, what with the ants itching me and all, even as I dozed. Coming down off the step to the bush I hid behind, he bent over and spread the branches. "And what would this be over here in the greenery?" His face—dead even with mine and inches only from it—woke me with a start.

Suddenly realizing the consequences of my actions, I couldn't speak, for if Jeremy were home, my father would not be far behind. "I'm too tired from slaving all day to come looking for the likes of you when I get home," he had said. My eyes grew wide now at the implications and I scrambled to my feet, ready to run.

Jeremy grabbed my arm. "Whoa now, just a minute. What is it that leads you to hide in the shrubs, I'm wanting to know?"

I pulled to get away. "I have to be home!"

"Have to be home, do you? Well then, why don't I come along with you, just to be sure you know the way?" Jeremy understood that I knew the way, for how else did I get there in the first place? It was the reason he was after. Before I knew it, he was walking and I was trotting down the sidewalk, spilling the beans about the kids in the neighborhood.

"Ah, the other ones is it that are bothering you? Well let's see what we can do about that."

Entering the corner store, Jeremy strode to the glass cabinet's display of penny candy. Now, I had already been to this place, stood in this very spot even, eyeing all the sweets that could be yours for a penny. A few days earlier I had been lucky enough to find a coin on the sidewalk and walked in big as life to buy a root beer barrel. But usually all I did was stand there and salivate.

Jeremy ordered a bag full of the best candies in the cabinet and paid the man sixty-three cents for sixty-three pieces of candy. Sixty-three! I did not know what he planned to do but I sure hoped they were meant for me.

"Now where are these friends of yours?" he asked as we walked out.

"They're not my friends."

He smiled. "They will be soon," he said, reaching his hand down as mine went up to meet it. A long time it had been since someone held my hand, and it felt infinitely wonderful.

"What are we going to do with the candy, Cousin Jeremy?"

"We're going to win you some friends, me little Aaron. We're going to win you some friends."

I thought he would just go to my street and give the candy to kids who promised to be my friend. I doubted that would work. They'd be nice with him around but when he was gone, they would-n't be any different than they were now. However, the plan old Cousin Jeremy had up his sleeve involved a little more than that.

In my excitement, I had forgotten my father's imminent arrival. Remembering, I hurried ahead to our corner. Many of the children had already been called into their houses for supper. Only a few still pushed rings or pulled wagons.

One tough kid who bullied me incessantly came ramming around the corner with one knee in his wagon, pushing with his other leg, and nearly brought us down. He swerved right into a pile of garbage cans, causing a terrible clatter.

Jeremy was over to help him out of the mess in a flash. I stood with my mouth open. I didn't like this kid and he didn't like me, that was the truth of it. But Jeremy dusted him off and said, "There now, that was close, wasn't it?" He asked if he was hurt, then checked his wagon to make sure it was all right.

The boy gleamed, recognizing a dandy.

"Say, what's your name?" Jeremy asked.

"Barney. What's your name, and who are you anyway?"

"I would be Jeremy Burke from that street over there. I also happen to be cousin to this young man, name of Aaron Burke."

Barney looked my way and wrinkled his nose. "I don't like him. He talks funny and don't smile none."

"And how is it 'e be talking any diff'rent than meself? We both come from Ireland, God bless 'er soul, and are one and the same, if yer askin' me," said Jeremy in an exaggerated brogue. "Now, do y' like *me*, Barney?" He looked the boy straight in the eye, defying him to cast aspersions in his direction.

"I like you. You're nice." He pointed at me. "He's an old poop, is what he is."

"Ah, so 't isn't the talk, then, that y' be reactin' to, is it? Well, let's see if Aaron over 'ere ever does smile."

He put his arm around Barney's shoulder, and they walked in my direction. I fought the urge to back up, not knowing what to expect. Jeremy frightened me a bit now, and I had the suspicious feeling he was going to put me on the spot.

I was right.

"Ah now, Aaron, do y' know this lad 'ere—Barney, isn't it?" he asked, looking first to Barney, then to myself. Barney looked up at him and nodded.

"I know who he is," I mumbled.

"What was that y' said, Aaron? I couldn't quite hear you."

"I know him," I said, louder this time.

"Well, Barney 'ere likes the way we talk, don't y', Barney?"

He had Barney trapped. If he said he didn't like the way we talked, he would disrespect Jeremy, whom he clearly did like. If he said he did like the way we talked, then it wouldn't be there for him to laugh at me when Jeremy was gone. What was a boy to do in a circumstance like this?

Cave in, of course.

"I. . .I like it well enough."

Jeremy laughed, patting us on our backs. As he did so, he moved us around so we stood next to each other facing him. "Ah, that's good t' hear, son, good t' hear." Made a pair of us he did, not against each other any longer but two boys on the same side.

He went and picked up the forgotten sack of delicacies he'd left on the walk when Barney tipped over. "So, now, what'll y' have, me Barney and me Aaron, for surely something good inside awaits its turn in yer mouths. Have a look 'n choose what y' like."

We brought our heads close together and looked into the prize bag.

"Ooh, it's candy, ain't it Mr. Jeremy?" In an instant however, his expression of happy surprise turned to disappointment. "My mom won't let me have candy before supper." Then he brightened. "But wait," he said, changing his mind, "do I see the buttons, Mr. Jeremy? Oooh! They're my favorite! Maybe if I save them for later, she won't mind," he said all in one breath.

Fast as Barney could think, his thoughts and any reasoning behind them were out. You knew what made the boy tick if you listened.

"Then the buttons it'll be." Jeremy gave me a wink. "And for you, Cousin Aaron, what would be your pick o' the evening?"

Jeremy's eyes twinkled upon my very being, but the word "evening" yanked me back to reality, and I made my choice a swift one. "I'll have the wrapped butterscotches in the bottom, thank you," I said, poking inside to reach them. I looked up into the happy eyes of Barney, who returned my grin.

"Pick what you like then. Best be off with you, Barney, for it'll be suppertime, won't it?"

"Yes sir, it will," and he scurried home.

"Now, Aaron, we'd best be on our way to your place before your father gets home. Won't be long now, I don't believe."

Indeed, wasn't that just him coming from the opposite direction? As Father drew closer, he frowned, no doubt noticing the leaves and dirt still clinging to my clothes. "And what might you two be doing out together on such an evening as this?" he asked when he was within earshot.

Jeremy flashed him the brightest of smiles. "Ah, 'twas a-visiting me he was, Uncle Edward, and a welcome sight it is to see young Aaron any time of day."

We entered the house, Father first, me last.

"Visiting you then, was it? And what would be the purpose of such a visit?" asked The Inquisitor.

"No purpose but to chat about life here in Chicago, Uncle Edward."

"Well, there's enough work around here for him not to go off looking to bother anyone else. Look at the pans where I left them last night, not even rinsed or sanded. Food out on the counter for flies and bugs to eat, as if we didn't need every morsel for ourselves. And what of the marketing? Did you get that done, boy, or are we to have another meal of Mrs. Meade's leftover garden vegetables? Just look at the place, dirt and dust everywhere, laying where it will."

Actually, the place looked like it always did.

"This is not the way to live, Aaron, my boy." He looked at Jeremy as he opened the door. "Jeremy, you'll have to excuse us. Aaron has shirked his chores once again and must take his punishment as well as finish them up."

Jeremy walked to the door, then turned. "Aaron, these are for you. Share with your friends. You'll find they appreciate a heart that is generous and true, no matter the words you speak." The bag of candy having passed to my hand, he was out the door.

Father shut it and turned on me. "Here now, what did he give you that your father has no knowledge of?" Taking the bag from my hands, he emptied it across the table. "What? Candy? What use is candy, when we're starving for real food, boy? If he were to buy us something, it should have been a side of beef or some fresh vegetables, not something as worthless as candy. I never saw the likes of such waste in my life. Surely our cousin is good-hearted, but frugality and wisdom come not his way, I'm a-thinking."

His face darkened. "If that man thinks he can win me own son away from me with sweets, he's got another thing coming. I'll not have you visiting him again, do you hear? I can take care of my own son, I can, without the help of others." He gathered the goodies from the table and dumped them into the slop jar. "There. That's what they're good for. Have not another thought about Jeremy nor his treats. They'll come to no good around here, for tear you away from me he will, then leave you on the doorstep when he's bored with you. Mark my words."

I knew what was coming and crept to the corner at his approach.

"And you, boyo! You've weaseled out of your duties once and for all." He grabbed me by the collar. "You left, it would appear, as soon as you found yourself food, with not a care for the house or what we'd need for evening." He gave my hair a good tug. "Look at me, when I speak to you. Not up to your chores, are you? Answer me, boyo."

"No, sir," I said, close to a whimper but not wanting him to thrash me for crying like a babe. Always wanting to toughen me up, he figured a good thrashing would do it if I cried. And I couldn't say, "Yes, sir," since that would be disagreeing with him.

He put on his hat. "Well then, we'll have to find something you are up to. Come after me," he commanded, stepping out into the night, dragging me with him by the shirtsleeve. I slipped and stumbled trying to keep up as his anger propelled us down the street.

We turned the corner in the direction opposite Jeremy's house. Two blocks later we reached the main street with its markets and dry goods stores. Jerking me by the ear at the end of the block, he swung me around the corner and into the livery.

"Evening," said the boy on duty, a curious expression on his face as he noted our manner of entry.

"Where would the owner be, if I may ask?"

"Mr. McCalloran will be having supper with his family, he will." He wasn't really a boy at all. More a youth with a good stocky build.

"Well, I got a mind to put my boy to work for him."

The lad eyed me, his doubt as to the worthiness of anything I could accomplish obvious.

"You'll have to see him in the morning, when he gets here. Can't do anything for you now, I'm afraid."

"Well, tell him Edward Burke wants to see him first thing, before the cock crows," and we were off again, backtracking our way to the flat.

I was ebullient! To be able to work with big people, do what they do, go where they go! Just think of it! I knew that boys my age did odd jobs, but never did I think my father would send me to a real job where they'd *pay money* for the likes of my services before he even had me in school.

My father, however, had another agenda. He opened our door and threw me in by the arm. Windmilling, I hit the wall hard, then slid onto my bottom. Tears ran down my cheeks. I could do nothing to stop them now.

"You! You're a waste! I don't know what possessed me to bring you along to this new life." He stomped through the house, lighting and trimming the lamps. "Look at you, a crybaby if ever I saw one."

I came out of that evening with bruises on my body but not my face, mind you, for didn't I have to be presentable the next day?

Before dawn, he pushed me to wake up. We went down to the livery where Mr. McCalloran was busy hitching up two fine looking bays.

"Boy tells me you got a wee one for the work," he said as we rounded the bend into the stable.

"He may be small, but he does a man's work, that he does. Trained him myself, I did, and he is capable." I had never heard my father say a good thing about me, and he said it in my hearing now only to get what he wanted. What training he spoke of, I did not know. I could work hard, that I could. But I doubted I could saddle a horse if my life depended on it.

Mr. McCalloran finished hitching the horses and turned to

look me over. "He's a might small for working the horses, I will say. About all he'd be good for would be cleaning and feeding. I suppose we could try him a day and see if he's up to it. If he is, he don't get paid for the trial. His workday will begin at five in the morning and end at seven in the evening. 'Tis a long day for a lad like this who should be in school, if he's even the age for that."

And that is how I began my first day of work.

❖   ❖   ❖

I rose early with my father thereafter and got right to pitching hay for Mr. McCalloran. The pitchfork towered over me, but I was a tough little rascal with much to prove to blokes that had me pegged as a "worthless little one." Pouring out the oats was not easy, that I'll tell you, for I had to pull the heavy bag behind me to each stall. The easiest part was cleaning, for it was not all that heavy to do. At that age I was too young to bridle or lead the horses in and out, but the animals moved aside for me if I asked them to when their stalls had to be cleaned.

I'd start talking before I even opened the gate. They could hear me and knew what was coming. Weren't stupid, you know, like some thought.

"Come on, now, Bridie," I'd say to the golden mare with the black mane. "Let's have a go at it."

She'd clomp around a little, excited I guess to have company in her stall. Or maybe she'd be glad to have it cleaned. Sometimes she'd snort or whinny just so I'd know she heard me. By the time I got the gate open—and wasn't that just the job for a boy my size—she'd be looking around at me, blinking her eyes.

"Move over now." As I brought the fork in, she'd move to the side. When I finished shoveling and pitching in fresh hay, I'd say something like, "All right now, let's do the other," and move right over she would. Easy as pie.

Most of the horses were boarded on a regular basis. Some only pulled wagons. Then there were the dandies kept as riding horses. More spectacular than plain workhorses, they also seemed more alive. If you had a life of hauling, you might be dulled out like the workhorses, too, don't you think? Where, if you had an owner that rode you and spoke to you and brought sweets for you, well, wouldn't you be happier?

People were that way, when they came for their horses. Those who drove the wagons were a different sort than the riders. The duller drivers came to life only in their camaraderie with each other, or when they lorded over the poor beasts of burden, snapping whips and pulling at bits. In their turn, I must say the horses sometimes responded in like manner, exhibiting a little life in their struggle to show who was boss. But it all came to naught, for they depended upon man for feeding and inevitably submitted to the drivers' cruelty.

Of course, that "man" who fed them now was me. Feeling I could change things for them a little if I liked, I began bringing them treats, especially to the ones I grew to love—and that wouldn't be the riding horses, either. Some of the workhorses had such velvety eyes, they melted my heart, and I gladly offered a bite of carrot or apple when I could find it. Poking my head out of the stall I'd just cleaned, I'd look up and down to be sure no one was coming. Then I'd hurry in, and that old horse—whichever one it was, because most of the workhorses were old—would already be nuzzling my pockets to see what I'd brought. They knew that if I came back in after cleaning, it was to bring a treat.

"Here you go," I'd whisper. She'd take it quick as a whip, and I'd be out and on to the next one. Liked me, they did.

Three years I stayed at this job. By the time I was about seven (I only knew my age by the passing seasons, guessing at the month and day of my birth), I could handle the bits and bridles. Using a footstool (meant for the ladies, I'm afraid), I was able to brush the horses down and blanket them when they came in. The only thing I was still too small to do was saddle them up.

The happiest part of life then was my work. I have seen this in many a person—time spent on the job makes sense, but time at home falls apart, for isn't it easier for some to earn a dollar than to please those in a household? It seemed so for me, at least.

My father showed up every Friday at 7 p.m. for my pay. "Hello, Mr. McCalloran," he'd bellow, all good will. "What's the good word?"

"Mr. Burke," the boss replied, nodding, "I expect you're wanting the boy's wages for the week." He knew what my father was about, all right. "Here you go."

What my father did with it, I'll never know, although many a Friday night I would awaken alone, only to hear him come in later smelling of the brew and something else I could not identify, though I think now it must have been the female scent. We slept in the same bed, and difficult it was not to notice strange or different odors.

Each night upon arriving home I completed my chores. Then we ate, cleaned up and went to bed, I before him. That is when he would go out. With me fast asleep, he could be off somewhere else. Many mornings, it was I who woke him out of a drunken slumber to get to work.

He was a dirty man, and I must have been dirty, too, for

though we changed to nightshirts at bedtime, we didn't bathe unless we paid a quarter for it at the bathhouse. We wore the same clothes all week. Three seasons out of the year, on our one day off—a different day for each of us—we rinsed them out in the lake. (Winters, we had to rinse them in the 'stern.) With him working in the cattle yards and me at the stable, we weren't the cleanest in Chicago.

Once working, I never did have time to play again with Barney and the neighborhood kids. We still saw Cousin Jeremy, but not often enough to suit me. Neecie and Johnny had us to their house for dinner one Sunday, but I think we stunk so badly she didn't want us inside after that. Any further invitations were for outings such as picnics or sledding.

It didn't matter to me what we did with Jeremy. Just to be around him was refreshment enough. Sometimes he pulled me aside to talk about getting into school, but Father was not about to budge off of liking the money I brought in. Jeremy finally saw the futility of it and put it to rest. On the other hand, more than once I saw my father talk with Jeremy in a low rumble—about what, I never knew until one of Neecie's picnics.

"Everyone gather 'round," Jeremy called. We dropped our croquet mallets and ran to where he stood next to my father. "Uncle Edward has an announcement to make."

Now, may I say I had noticed changes in my father lately? Grumpy and more irritated than normal one moment, he would shift without notice to something approaching frivolity. In our household, that was a marked change. So when Jeremy called us, I knew something was up. I just didn't know what.

"We're going to be moving out of the area, Aaron and me," Father said.

I was stunned. I did not necessarily like our living circum-stances, but I had made a place for myself at my work and was pleased with what I could do. Plus, it helped to know that Jeremy was close by.

"We've been hearing at the yards about great opportunity to the north of here. I'm going to go have a look around and see if there mightn't be land for the taking."

This brought a great response from the group. Everyone had seen the ships stacked with timber from Northern Michigan for the building going on in Chicago, their crews telling stories of great tracts of land up for grabs. The land cleared of timber would make good farmland for some lucky blokes who didn't mind the cold.

"Opportunity knocks up there, for it's just now being devel-oped. Ain't nothing like this place where people have been around for awhile," he said. "They're telling of the blackest soil you ever saw, places where you can grow anything, pastures where cattle eat all they want, clean lakes and streams full of fish…and the loggers have already cleared the land, so you can get right to plowing! I want to be one of the smart ones moving to this new land."

Another move. I wondered if Jeremy would be along as I sighed and withdrew from the crowd to sit under a large maple.

He must have sensed my thoughts, for he came to sit next to me and picked a long blade of grass, slipping it between his lips to chew. "Ah, Aaron, 'tis a fine thing your father's doing. The land will be clean and new for you."

"Are you coming, Jeremy?"

"Nay, I won't be able to accompany you, I'm afraid, for have you not noticed? I've taken up with Neecie's younger sister over there. Asked for her hand, I did. I plan on speaking with her father about it tonight. We'll make our home here for the time being, then see how we are about it." Jeremy had a fine job as a skilled journeyman doing finish work on cabinets and banisters and the like in the more elegant Chicago homes. I doubted there would be such fine houses going up in the unsettled land Up North.

We gave two weeks' notice and cleaned out of the flat that I won't say I called "home." It would be a long time until I would feel comfortable enough to call a place home, but that time would come.

Aye, that it would.

6

MAUDIE
Michigan, 1894

Off we were to yet another new land where we could begin again.
Age seven I was, and craving more than anything just to have a
place to live that would feel like home used to.

I still thought of Mummy. She came to me when I closed my
eyes at night, and I would talk with her and tell her my fears and
problems and sometimes cry because I couldn't feel her arms
'round me. To be able to talk in your head with anyone at all is a
wondrous thing, but a child needs the warmth and touch of a
mother's love physically. 'Tis a thing to cause the world to grieve,
when a child does not have the mother-love. It does terrible things
inside both mother and child when they are separate. I was never
to be like other people. There were many reasons for it, but this
was a big one.

Our things piled on the back of a wagon pulled by a work-
horse purchased from my former employer, we journeyed the
rough roads up the eastern coast of Lake Michigan. Stopping at
night in the countryside, we made our beds outside, whatever the
weather. One time, we bedded underneath the wagon, so heavy

was the rainfall and hail. We traveled this way a fortnight or so, asking in the towns about land for sale as we drew farther north.

I had no idea how far north or south we were, but I did notice a change in the air. It seemed fresher, and the land became sandy in some places, full of trees in others—where they still stood, that is, for hadn't the loggers done a fine job of flattening them all around? Rolling stump-covered hills said we were getting there, for true logging country is what the sailors had told us about, after all. Coming to a port called Ludington, my father continued on. Land prices might be lower the farther we went. We passed Frankfort, a port not quite as busy as Ludington, and were almost there. Three ports up, he decided this was it.

Now, I did not know all this because my father told me, but from conversations he had with others along the way—travelers, merchants, workers at the docks. Listening was the only way I could keep a finger on what was happening: where we were going, what we were looking for, how long it would take. For when we traveled alone on the road, the two of us never spoke.

We made camp outside the port of Glen Haven. My father spent the days in town, gathering information. Sometimes we rode around the area on the horse together, but usually he left me at the camp to fill my days. Since we were not far from town, I meandered in and out as I liked, observing people.

It was a pretty place, was Glen Haven. Bustling, too. Ships docked at the harbor, loading lumber and bringing in supplies. Some, destined for more distant ports, came in during bad weather, as high hills protected the bay on three sides. The bay's western arm was actually all golden sand. They called it the "sand dunes." Vegetation and trees grew at the base of the dunes, but the top glowed yellow and beautiful against the blue water. Trees covered the eastern arm of the bay, the loggers' great slashes everywhere. Straight out from the dock, two blue and white islands sat on the horizon.

My father finagled a large piece of land over the hills away from town with a cabin on it already, built perhaps by loggers or a trapper before them. Situated by a creek, our new home sat surrounded by stump-covered hills. He bought a mule, and we spent our days removing the stumps, roots and all. I led the beast, and he would be behind, wedging under each one to get it out. Hard work it was, and for what, he never did tell me until he plowed the field under the next spring and planted corn.

Father had me clear stones from the fields; hold up logs he placed for the fences we made; feed the animals (we started with two, but soon had more); and clean the outbuildings, once built, when they got bad. He worked hard, too, but did take time for himself, leaving me in the night to go into town for a hand of cards or to see what ladies might be had.

As a boy, I could not appreciate the beauty of this place. We lived among the hills and lakes that were to become a true home for me many years later, but while I lived with this man, a refuge it could never be. Nothing about life rated highly for me in those days. We had little contact with others, never heard from our homeland, and even lost touch with Jeremy.

Few were the women not already saddled with husband and family in that neck of the woods, yet find one he did, not at night but at the dry goods store one day. I was along to help with the loading, and father had me wait as usual with the horse and wagon outside. Forever, it seemed until he exited the place with a woman who appeared to be quite a bit older than him.

Dashing, he bowed as he held the door, saying, "Allow me."

Never had I seen my father behave in such a manner.

She laughed and responded, "Why thank you, kind sir."

They bantered back and forth, and before we left he gained himself an invitation to call the following Sunday.

Her name was Mrs. Whitcomb. My father called on her each Sunday for a month, then brought her out one Saturday in late spring after the corn had sprouted and was looking rather good, this being our third year. That would put me around the age of ten, close as I can tell. We worked hard that week, mending fences and cleaning up the yards round the place.

I can't say I have ever seen my father get nervous. It would be my guess that if he were so, it would come out in a gruffness. So the inordinately irritated way he ordered me around that morning gave me to think that this visit of Mrs. Whitcomb's was more important to him than he would have me believe.

When he left to fetch her, he sent me inside to scrub the kitchen, sweep the floor and clean myself up. There wasn't much to be done inside the cabin, such as it was. Plank flooring and a stone foundation held up the walls around the place. We had stoned in a good chimney and fireplace the year before, and— though the windows were few, the appointments scarce, and the furniture handmade for the most part—it had been good enough for my father and me. There was not much to clean.

I sat wondering what it all might mean when I heard their wagon approach. As they drove up, I walked onto the porch. My father hopped down and ran around to help Mrs. Whitcomb, who was already on the ground making her way to me.

She greeted me in the kindest fashion. "How I admire the work you have done here with your father, young man," she said as she looked at the land around the house. I squinted to look up into her face, but the sun glared behind her head, and I couldn't get a good look under her bonnet. She was dressed plainly and cleanly though, that I could see. And she was large, that I could see, too, as I stretched my hand out to meet her gloved one. Taking mine in hers, she patted it with the other. She turned to speak to my father, and I saw her face for the first time up close. I would call it comfortable. She, too, squinted up into the sunlight to look at my father who had come to stand just behind her. His teeth gleamed as he smiled that Big Smile he used when he wanted people to be nice to him.

"That'd be my boy, Aaron," he said, as if he were proud. I thought he might just be using me to get closer to this woman as he had done with Jeremy years before, for it was easy to see that she did in fact approve of me.

As this was our third spring, we had gotten to know most of the people in our small town. Mrs. Whitcomb lost her husband to the fever that had been rampant before we arrived and lived in town, working at a boardinghouse for another man and his wife who were getting on in years themselves. She was a hard worker and pleasant enough—two qualifications that made her a good candidate for my father. I had seen him tip his hat to her in the past, but it took all this time for him to know her well enough to begin courting her, I guess. He needed her help at the farm, and she was able-bodied—that we could both see.

Nobody mentioned Mummy. I didn't know but that you couldn't have a new wife if you lived in a new country, and I didn't dare meddle and ask. It wasn't until later that this would become a problem.

Mrs. Whitcomb came into our home and changed our lives. On Saturdays, she brought pies and bread she had baked, sweetening up the place with flowers from her garden. We went to her home on Sundays for dinner after Mass, which we began attending after father met her. It wasn't that father believed, but she thought it important, and his goal was to win her over.

I loved going to her house. Sunday dinner cooked while we were at church, so her home always smelled of good things to eat when we arrived. Lovely ornamental items called to your insides, they were so pretty. Little lace doilies were spread out like cloth snowflakes everywhere, and on darker days, the polished furniture reflected the light cast by pretty lamps.

After several months of back and forth visits, it was obvious to everyone in town what was happening, and early the following spring, wedding bells chimed for my father and Mrs. Whitcomb, who was now "Mrs. Burke."

That posed a problem for me.

After the wedding, I sat next to her at the little church reception. She laughed at something one of her friends said, then turned to me. "Well, now, Aaron. What do you think of all this?"

"I think it's fine, Mrs. Whitcomb." I was really quite happy that this woman would be in our home all the time now. Perhaps my father would be kinder with her around.

Her expression changed to surprise, then she laughed. "What? Mrs. Whitcomb?"

I slumped down, embarrassed at my mistake.

"I'm sorry, Aaron, but I'm Mrs. Burke now," she said, smiling to her friends who all nodded their approval. But then concern clouded her face. "Oh, Aaron," she murmured close to my ear. "What would you like to call me? I'm no longer Mrs. Whitcomb, and you can hardly call me Mrs. Burke."

I wasn't going to call her "Mother." That was for sure.

She paused, then brightened. "I know! Why don't you call me

what your papa does?" He called her "Maudie," short for Maude. "Does that feel good to you?"

I smiled at the idea of calling her a grownup name. Nodding my head, I straightened up and said, "It feels all right." So "Maudie" it was.

Maudie soon had a pet name for me—"Ronie." You see, my father pronounced my name with the accent on the second syllable, making it sound like the word for the type of horse called a "roan," so the name sounded like "ah-ROAN." Others pronounced it however they liked, but this was the old Irish way, and Maudie knocked off the first syllable, adding the diminutive "ee" sound to the end of it as Americans were so fond of doing. But instead of making me feel diminished, I felt more special.

When Maudie came to stay with us that spring, she quit her job at the boardinghouse and closed up her house in town for the season. In the fall, we opened up the house in town and stayed there for the winter. Come time for plowing, out again to the farm we would go.

Having Maudie at the farm all the time changed the way we lived even more. She brought furniture out from her house—nice things—even some that had belonged to her first husband, like a good rocking chair and a few pipes for Father. She brought out quilts for the cool nights—and a special one just for me, since the three of us wouldn't be sharing the one bed we had, nor one room anymore, either.

That spring before the wedding, we had added my room and a sitting room off the kitchen for guests. Maudie had friends—a lot of them—and call they would on Sundays, which were for church, family and social visits. Most people worked the rest of the week, and farmers worked Sundays, too. But the ladies kept social times going even if the men were out in the fields.

Life with Maudie meant she did many of the chores I used to, but it also meant that my father and I had to change some of our ways. "What's acceptable to the two of you is not necessarily acceptable to the likes of me!" she scolded one Saturday night soon after the wedding. "I'll not have ladies coming to visit a pigsty!" Father and I learned to clean up more to Maudie's liking, for when we let it go a bit, we heard about it.

It didn't take long after their marriage for Maudie to see the kind of man my father really was, though, and how he treated me. Things didn't change as much as I had hoped after all. I remember him ranting and raving about my oafishness one evening at supper.

"And then I goes into the barn, and what do you think I see?"

She looked at him, waiting.

He gestured toward me. "This one here, over in the corner astrokin' the cow's head as if she's the apple of his eye. Now how do you like that? A boy who wastes his time talking to animals, instead of caring for them!"

"Oh, Edward, don't you think. . ." she began.

"Think nothing!" He pushed his chair back and the table forward as he stood to make his point. "This place needs tending, and myself and this little squirt over here are the only ones to do it. If the animals don't get fed, they die." He looked at me. "And he knows it, too, he does."

I looked down at my plate. Truth be told, I *had* been finding comfort with the animals. I loved them.

"Sometimes," continued my father—not for the first time in my hearing, but Maudie hadn't heard it before, "I regret the day I brought you here, boyo. I didn't have to do it, you know. Was the good of me heart that brought you over to keep you from starving. And look at the thanks I get. In fact," my father bent over to look into my eye which was as close to the plate as possible, "I ain't never heard a word of thanks." He strode off into the sitting room. "Show's that what I do for you is a waste, just a waste." He got his coat and slammed the door as he left for the barn.

Maudie and I sat at the table, neither of us saying much. Soon, she took up her silver and speared a piece of potato. "Eat, Ronie. You need your fuel."

But I couldn't, not with the knowledge that any minute he could come through that door again, making more accusations.

"Ronie, I see how it is with you and your father, and I'm sorry for it."

Her words pierced the heavy wall that shut all feeling from my heart, and tears slipped down my cheeks.

"There, now, Aaron," she said, coming over to put her arm across my shoulder. But I couldn't have that. What if Father came in and saw her comforting me after what he'd said? Plus, if she comforted me any more than she already had, the dam inside me might break wide open, and I'd be bawling till Kingdom Come. So I ran to my room, shut the door, buried my head in my pillow and cried my eyes out anyway.

Maudie tried to take me under her wing, but I was standoff-ish. Alone for too long to be able to warm up easily to anyone, I rarely spoke with her, especially after my shameful display of emotion. She asked me about myself, but what was there to tell? I was there to help my father. That was my life. If I had any interests, like the look in the animals' eyes when I fed them, I kept such things to myself, for they seemed ridiculous even to me.

Yet the woman continued to do special things for me. I had always worn hand-me-downs we got at the church back door, but now she mended our garments, made me a shirt and pants for church, and knitted socks and sweaters for the winter. And she cooked good food. We appreciated the change in our diet, for long had we eaten only the simplest things to make.

Soon after taking up residence with us, Maudie inquired into my schooling. The children in the area went to a small public school run by a good man by the name of Mr. Bowen. Maudie asked Mr. Bowen to come see us one evening without asking my father's permission, since she had already broached the subject with him, and he would have none of it. But when Mr. Bowen learned I had no education whatsoever, he indicated it might be difficult for me to fit in.

"Most of the children began their education at the age of six," he explained. "Aaron here is eleven already, going on twelve. He would not catch up to the others for several years, Maude."

Then he turned to me. "Aaron, you would be at the same level as the youngest students. I don't think you'd be comfortable in that situation, do you?"

Mightily disappointed, I don't think I answered yea or nay.

"I can take you in, if that's what you want, but I wouldn't advise it."

He turned back to Maudie. "It might be better if you and the boy's father taught him. I could bring out books and other materials, and you could school him here. Many people do it that way, and I think you'd feel more comfortable, Aaron, too."

Obviously, the man didn't grasp the unlikelihood of my father helping me with anything. Besides, I doubted my father knew much about reading or writing.

But Maudie surprised me. "I'll help him. And we'll have a grand time doing it!" she exclaimed, giving my knee a pat.

Thus we began my education in my twelfth year. I had never written anything and found it difficult to school my fingers into holding a small writing instrument and make tiny markings on the slate. Maudie said I was a quick learner, but I think it might just have been that I was so old when I started, my brain took in more. In addition, hadn't I already observed many of the things she taught, so I could relate to them more quickly than younger children? At any rate, I moved out of the first books and into thicker ones rapidly.

It turns out we could only do schooling in the winter, for during farming season I was out in the fields all day and too exhausted at night for studying. This could have limited my progress as a student, but what educational work I accomplished was easily done, and I advanced swiftly. It seems I had an aptitude for letters and numbers—was quite good at it, actually—and I enjoyed it, especially when I began to read things I hadn't known about.

But my father disapproved of the whole idea. "If you can count out your money, that's all you'll be needing," he would say. "Know how much seed you need, and that'll be enough. I won't have such foolishness as book learning for myself, and you'd be smart to spend your time learning a trade rather than having your nose stuck in a book every night." He would move in a huff to another part of the house to clean a tool or whatever while Maudie and I worked together.

She and I had a good time at it. She was very encouraging, and I began to open up and trust her. We laughed a lot.

"Oh, Ronie!" she would exclaim over some small accomplishment. "Look at what you can do! For the likes of me, I never saw a child learn so quickly."

Finally, I could do something and do it well. It felt almost as good as my work had in Chicago. I would have to say that this is the happiest I had been since living with my mother and siblings back in Ireland.

As time went on, my father became less agreeable with Maudie, falling back to the way he had always been with me and the others we left behind so long ago.

One day, I came into the farmhouse to find a tool for him and heard Maudie bawling in the bedroom. I went to her door. "Maudie?" I asked, not wishing to disturb her if she didn't want to be interrupted.

"Oh, Ronie, I'm sorry. I'm such an old fool," she said, wiping tears away with a dishtowel she had brought from the kitchen. "I didn't want you to see me like this."

"What's wrong, Maudie?" Now, I knew plenty was wrong, for hadn't I heard the arguments they were beginning to have—arguments strangely familiar, hailing back to my youngest days? And didn't Father sometimes storm out in the evenings, not returning until late into the night, banging his way into the house and into her room, rousing her with his meanness? Barely old enough had I been to recall the first times, yet there they were, stuck way back in my being. Now the horror of that time and of the way it ended returned. I was living the nightmare all over again.

"Maudie, can I help you?" I didn't know what I could possibly do; but by God, if there were something, I would do it.

"Ah, nothing can help me, Aaron. But something, or rather, *someone* can help you, and that would be me." She sat up, her eyes blazing. "I'm gonna get you out of here someday, Ronie, so you can have a good life of your own away from him. I see the way of it for you, and he'll use us both up, if we're not careful. There's nothing to do about it for me. I'm too old to work for anyone other than

Polinski's boardinghouse, and they've already taken another maid. But you have a life ahead of you, and I'll not sit and watch it wasted away by this tyrant you call your father and I now call my husband."

I sat down on the edge of the bed, my knees weak. I had thought I'd be here forever—that my entire existence was only for my father's keeping. Hadn't he told me over the years that I was good for nothing else? But Maudie had shown me I might be brighter than I believed. Now she was saying that I could make a living for myself away from my father!

"You'll have to get as far from him as you can so he won't come and get you. But first, you must learn your reading and writing and numbers. We'll work on that real hard and keep the reason a secret, you and me. For if he were to find out, it would be the end of the letters for you, and who knows what it would be like in this household for the two of us?"

Maudie's eyes filled with fear and bravery at the same time. "Promise me you'll not breathe a word of what I've just said, Aaron." She leaned forward, looking right into my being. "Do you promise?"

I swallowed, then took an oath I would live up to if it killed me. "I promise not to say anything," I vowed, then wondered. "Do you really think I could get away and find something to work at myself?"

"You're a bright boy, Aaron. You'll have to be older, but there is much you can do. Don't you already have more experience than most boys your age, with all the work you've done? The only thing they have over you is the learning, and we're working on that."

Heavy footsteps tramped up the porch stairs. I jumped off the bed, stepped out of the room and rummaged around for the tool

I was supposed to have found. Maudie got up, wiped her face, freshened the bed and came out of the room, her face puffy, her eyes red and watery.

"What's going on here?" my father asked, looking first at Maudie, then at me and back at her.

"My own clumsiness is all, Edward. I stumbled over the rocker and hurt my leg. But Aaron here brought me a cool cloth, and it's better now."

I beamed at her. She met my eyes briefly, then cast hers down to straighten her skirt as she moved to her chores in the kitchen once more. We had a new purpose in life, did Maudie and me— to get me ready for the big wide world.

7

FREEDOM
Michigan, 1902

Things did not go well for the farm in my fifteenth year. A blight on the crops that spring, then a drought in the summer, resulted in a less than fair yield at harvest-time, and I was forced to look for work outside the household for the second time in my life. By everyone's account, I was more than old enough.

A little grocery run by an older couple in nearby Empire needed a stock boy, and that turned out to be me. Getting that job brought responsibility along with plenty of praise, for hadn't my father drummed the work ethic into me? I had hardly done anything *other* than work all my short life in America. I knew that if I didn't do what I was told, I would pay for it dearly at home. So when I went to work for someone else, instead of a lackadaisical youth, they found an honest, hard worker.

I performed my duties well for Maudie's sake, too. She had dedicated herself to my upbringing and learning, and now it was my turn to take care of her. When payday came, I turned it all over to my father except for a little I held back and gave to Maudie. She thanked me with a glow, and put it away somewhere, for what purpose I did not care. It was for her that I gave it.

You see, my father had become ruthless at home. We were his servants. But Maudie and I banded together, helping each other in whatever ways we could. Made it bearable, it did, and I've never forgotten the bond that grew between us.

I stowed a little of my pay away for myself as well; kept it in the barn in a burlap bag, along with items I'd begun to gather for my future. I would go out in the dead of winter, climb up to the hayloft, dig under the hay and bring out my bag. A horse blanket thrown over my shoulders, I would count and figure what I would need.

Made some acquaintances among the other fellows in town, I did, while working at the grocery. Matt Stewart and Abel Chapman would come in after school and chat every now and again. Their families were merchants in the village, so they were always to be seen around town, hanging out in front of the barbershop or down by the hardware store. When they needed food, their mothers sent them over to us.

We were not all that familiar with each other—I knew who they were, just didn't really *know* them—and I filled their bills quietly and self-consciously. Keeping an eye on them from under my cap as I gathered their goods, I admired their happy-go-lucky attitudes.

Before long, they began coming in with girls on their arms, giggling and laughing over some tomfoolery. These boys were the life of the party, attracting everyone with their handsome youthfulness, their fun, their stylish ways of walking about town. But I became more self-conscious. As I left them by the cash register to fill their bills, they would look my way and murmur something to their girlfriends. Then everyone would snicker. I knew they made jokes about me. I could read well enough to fill bills and count well enough to make change, but having never been in a school-room, I didn't talk or act like them. I was a bit different, lacking the socializing you get in a schoolroom filled with other children.

Soon, I dreaded the times they came into the store. I withdrew further, attracting even more attention to my odd ways. They giggled more, I became more resentful, and the day came when I could bear it no longer.

Abel came into the store all dandied up in his school clothes, a girl on each arm. I stood behind the counter.

"Well, hello there, Mickey," he said.

"Name's Aaron," I muttered. They knew my name.

"Oh, yeah, I forgot."

The girls tittered.

"Hey, we need these, and *pronto*." He slapped a list on the counter and pushed it toward me.

The bell on the door rang and in came Matt with his admirers.

"Well, well, well," he said, tipping his cap to the ladies on Abel's arm. "Look what the cat dragged in." He gave his buddy a surly smile but winked at the girls.

"May I help you?" I asked Matt.

"You might be able to. Then again, you might not," he answered.

The girls laughed as if the remark had been clever.

I took his order along with Abel's and searched up and down the aisles, a basket over my arm, filling their orders. When I finished, I brought it all to the front, separated it into two piles, figured them and handed each his bill.

"Ahem." This was Abel. "I believe there is a mistake here." He pointed to the total on his bill, which I had already checked backwards. It was right.

"Why," said Matt in mock amazement, "there's a mistake on mine, too!"

The girls smirked as they pretended to be serious.

"And where is that mistake?" I asked.

"You can't see it?" asked Matt. "It's right in front of your face!" He pushed my head down hard on top of the bill on the counter, squishing my nose. They ran out the door and down the street, hallooing and raising a ruckus for the whole town to hear. The girls followed at a more sedate pace, giggling at the antics of the two ruffians.

I threw away both bills, replaced the goods on the shelves, and resolved I would never serve those boys again. Ever! After closing, I stomped back to Maudie's and rushed to my room, throwing myself face down on the bed. It was all so frustrating! I pounded the pillow with my fist and had a nice fight with it.

Maudie came right into my room from making supper without a knock or a call.

"Here, now, what's this?" she asked, and I looked up in surprise, my face streaked with tears. I thought I had drowned my words by stuffing my head in the pillow, but the house was small and hear me she did.

"What's the matter, Ronie?"

"I hate them!" I said, bashing in the pillow.

"Who now? Who do you hate?"

"Matt Stewart and Abel Chapman and all their friends, that's who!" I punched the pillow for each name as I said it.

"Why? What's happened?"

"They're always making fun of the way I talk or how I dress or act. They don't think I know anything because I'm not in school. And the girls laugh when the boys mimic me. I hate them all!"

"How long has this been going on?"

"Long as I've been working there. But the more they know me, the worse it gets. I thought at first we could be friends, but I was wrong, wrong, wrong!" Bang, bang, bang! on the pillow.

"I see," said Maudie.

"I'll never fit in with them. Never! And I don't want to, either!"

"Ah, so that's the way of it then," said my father, moving into the doorway behind Maudie.

"Father!" I sat up and dried my eyes. Hadn't heard him come and didn't like him catching me bawling my eyes out—me, a big lad of almost fifteen.

"Well, better to stay away from that sort anyway," he said. "Won't do you a bit of good to get mixed up in their shenanigans. Stay around here, and you won't get into any trouble." He walked away without realizing that I *always* got into trouble "around here."

I was trapped.

Maudie closed the door, came over and sat next to me. "I think it's time," she whispered.

We made our plans in earnest now. I had hidden away what money I could, and Maudie produced every penny I ever gave her, laying it out on my bedspread.

"Maudie! This was supposed to be for you!"

"No, Ronie. You're a generous soul, but what good can it do me? Buy me a new dress or a new pair of shoes? Oh, and they would be lovely to have, don't get me wrong. But I don't need them."

She didn't want my money. What little I had to give her sat upon the bedspread, and she didn't want it.

"But," she explained, "though this money can't change *my* circumstances, it could help *you* a great deal."

I looked up at her. What was she saying?

"Take this money and keep it someplace safe. Put other money with it as you can, and when the weather is warmer, my Ronie," she said with a vast and somber look in her eye, "I think it will be time for that life of your own we've been readying you for."

"That soon?" I didn't feel ready. But I couldn't take much more of Matt Stewart and Abel Chapman, either. We'd end up in a fist-fight for sure.

"Well, it's February, and you ought to leave around the first of April. If you're to be packing before long, there's much to do."

"But where would I go?"

"How about that family of your mother's back in Boston?"

In the past year, we had received a letter from Jeremy in Chicago. I don't know how he found us, but he sent it to our town, care of General Delivery in my father's name, telling of my mother's demise. It seems she never got over our leaving, had never really been the same afterward, the life dwindling out of her over the years until none was left.

It also said that one of her sisters, my Aunt Louise, had moved to Boston with my uncle and cousins a few years ago. Before we left Ireland, they had all talked about coming to Boston. Perhaps that is how my father got the idea. Maybe he thought better of it once we got there knowing that other family might follow, and that's why we moved west as quickly as possible.

Maudie got the letter from the postbox and innocently opened it. You can imagine the upheaval in our home when it arrived. She became sick upon reading it, for it meant that the marriage she had been partner to had been a sham.

My father could see the bad way it put us with the townspeople, should they find out. He claimed innocence. "How was I supposed to know you can't have wives in different countries?" he asked, echoing my own reasoning, but Maudie knew better. He had betrayed her.

In those days, a woman's reputation had to be saved at all costs, so they sent for the priest, who annulled the first marriage and performed a second in the privacy of our home. That made it all right legally for Maudie, but she never trusted my father again. The only reason she remarried him was to save her reputation. Either way, her life was ruined.

The letter's effect on me was even worse. I had thought my mother still in Ireland and that I might be with her again someday. But now she was gone from the face of the earth, and except for Maudie, I was truly alone. I grieved all that year for my mother and my loss of family, which is why Maudie thought I should go and seek my mother's people in Boston when the time came.

Not wanting to arouse Father's suspicion meant that anything I packed for the trip would have to be gathered and kept surreptitiously. There was much sneaking and creeping about as Maudie and I conspired together. When we went to the store, we got something extra. At home, Maudie worked on spare socks or a shirt or pants—something more than usual. It worked to our advantage that he paid us little heed. If he found out, he would take everything and chuck it.

We fixed up a nice bundle, and when spring came, I said

goodbye. My father was at the farm mending plows and hitches for spring planting, though we hadn't moved there yet. I was supposed to be at work, but instead, Maudie wrapped up my knapsack. She put in jerkied meat, bread, some cheese and dried fruit to get me started.

I filled my canteen at the pump and turned to her. "Maudie, what will happen when he comes home?"

She brushed away my concern with a flip of her hand. "Bah! I'll be just as surprised as he!" Hug me, she did, her eyes glistening. "You'd best get away while you have the chance, Ronie," she said, patting my hat on my head. She gave me a buss on the cheek, too, surprising me. I hadn't been kissed since I was a wee one.

I left through the back gate and walked the side roads where no one would wonder where I was going with such a large pack on my back and tears in my eyes. Miles down the road I realized I might never see this town nor these two ever again.

As I walked south through the woodlands and past the swamps of Michigan, the embryo of an idea took shape in my head that perhaps my mother was not dead. Maybe Jeremy hadn't gotten the story right, and she was alive. That thin thread of hope enticed me all the way to Boston. I hitched rides from farmers trundling to towns I had never heard of, slept nights by the highway, and soon bought a ticket for the second train ride of my life.

"Where're ya headed, sonny?" asked the ticketmaster.

"Boston, sir! One ticket for Boston!"

My life my own at last, I enjoyed the ride, watching passengers and scenery equally. Though still absorbed in my problems, I appreciated the fact that I was free of my father. One month after leaving Glen Haven, I entered the city I had passed through eleven years before on the very same railroad line.

Now the real task of finding my mother's family began. Her sister married a man named Sean O'Sullivan. Jeremy's second letter said the O'Sullivans lived in the Irish sector where he lived when we met him.

I had struck up a correspondence with Jeremy, proud to write a letter with Maudie's help. "Where would that Irish sector be?" I wrote, hinting that I might one day retrace our steps.

Jeremy answered that his section of the city had been torn down. "But if you ever go to Boston, look up my brother, Tom. He knows everyone in town," and he enclosed Tom's address.

I thought myself well equipped to find my mother's people, but when I found Tom's house, no one was home. I went to the nearest pub, knowing that some Irish in any neighborhood might frequent such places. Although the bartend was not ready to admit me for a drink, when I asked about Tom Burke, he let me in. The patrons lit up and told me many tales, laughing as they did, for Tommy was as well-liked as his brother. I listened, smiling at their jokes, holding in my impatience. I was so close!

Then I asked about the O'Sullivans, and finally one old bloke said, "Sean O'Sullivan and his family live a mile or so to the west, I believe."

"On Canterbury Street," added another, giving me general directions, and off I went. After asking the way a few times from passersby, I stood in front of a house on a maple-lined street, thinking for the first time how dirty and mussed up I must look. But, gathering courage, I opened the gate, walked up to the door and rang the bell.

It chimed inside, and a woman's voice called, "I'll get it."

She opened the door. Her presence smacked me hard in the chest. Auburn hair. Face of a porcelain doll. Dressed in green, with one hand on the doorknob, she held herself in an easy pose.

Vaguely, I noticed an older woman peer out from behind her.

"Yes?" asked the younger woman.

I had found her. "Mother?" I asked.

The older woman's face blanched. Her brows rose, her jaw dropped, and her eyes rolled back into her head as she fell to the floor in a dead faint.

8

FAMILY

Boston, 1902

The young woman at the door turned around. "Mama!" she cried, stooping down. "Mama, what's wrong?"

The older woman groaned, and her eyes fluttered open. Her gaze sharpening, she looked out at me still on the step, horrified.

"Tell him to come in," she whispered.

"Mama, are you all right?"

"Tell him."

The younger one turned to look at me with eyes fearful and wary. "Come in."

I was wrong. My mother would never look at me that way. Besides, this woman was too young to be Mummy. How foolish I must seem. Woodenly, I stepped over the threshold.

"Please, Kathleen," said the mother, "let's shut the door." She sat up with an effort and looked at me again. "Well."

I found my tongue. "I'm sorry, ma'am."

"Aaron."

She knew who I was!

"We thought you dead."

I couldn't reply. Why would they think me dead?

"Mama? You know this boy?"

"Aye, but I've not seen him since he was a wee one. It is Aaron, is it not?"

"Yes, ma'am, it is," I replied.

"Ah, now," she stood with her daughter's assistance, "don't be calling your Aunt Louise 'ma'am.' We're family, aren't we." It was a statement.

Dear God.

Steadying herself with one hand on her daughter's shoulder, Aunt Louise straightened her dress. "This is your cousin, Kathleen. And doesn't she look like your poor mother? No wonder you called her that."

Kathleen and I looked at each other, putting the pieces together, figuring out where I belonged in the clan. She must have known about me at one time.

"Kathleen, say hello to your cousin, Aaron."

Kathleen offered her hand, her eyes no longer wary, just curious. "H'llo, Aaron."

I took it, stiff with the strangeness of the situation. "H'llo."

I don't know what I expected. This was as far in my head as I could have possibly imagined. Up till now, what these people would think and do with me had been the least of my worries. Just trying to find them, coupled with thinking of my mother, had enveloped me to this point. I realized how senseless it had been not to consider the effect my appearing on their doorstep would have on them. Now that it had happened, there was nothing to do but go forward.

"Aaron," said my aunt, "leave your pack by the door."

I followed her into a side room at the front of the house. It looked ever so comfortable after my long journey.

"Please sit down, Aaron. Kathleen, fetch us some tea. I think we need it."

Kathleen, watching me, turned and went to the kitchen. She really did bring my mother's image fully back into my head, and I wanted to look at her more than was polite.

Some scuffling in the hall, and two heads peeked around the corner. Kathleen rounded up what must have been her siblings and sent them upstairs, chattering about the newly found cousin.

"Ah, Aaron. Aaron. Where have you been all these years, child? We'd lost all hope of ever finding you." Aunt Louise looked very tired.

"My father and I've been in Michigan, m'lady."

"So all these years, you've been over here." She looked sorrowful. "Ah, Aaron, had we only known."

"Aye."

It made me wonder why I had never thought to try to contact my family in Ireland. Of course, in Chicago, I hadn't been able to write. And to ask anyone else. . .Well, it might have gotten back to my father, and then what would have happened? Plus, I would have had to dictate such a letter, letting the transcriber know the exact circumstances of our situation. Would that have been so bad? Jeremy thought my mother had been the one to leave us. Ah, such a mess.

Her eyes were sad, her voice gentle. "Aaron, you do know that your mother is gone?" It was the death knell for the hope spinning me forward in my journey.

"Aye." The bottom fell out of me, and the top began to close over.

Aunt Louise wasn't about to let that happen. "Ah, but Aaron!"

she said. "You're alive! This is cause for celebration, for you're with us again! And we're so happy to have you here!"

Kathleen brought in the tea. Picking up the spark in her mother's words, she said, "Aye, we're glad to have you, Cousin Aaron. Look how far you've traveled!" she exclaimed, indicating my attire.

"Oh!" I had forgotten all about how I must look.

Both women laughed, and I relaxed and smiled, just beginning to comprehend the meaning of family.

That began one of the happiest times of my life. Aunt Louise and Kathleen settled me in the finest fashion, giving me a room of my own—the "garret," they called it—at the top of the house, with a fine feather mattress and a nice downy pillow. Helping me clean up my things, they exclaimed over the fine pieces Maudie had made, and listened to the stories I told of how she had helped me, about Father and our trip over from Ireland, of Chicago and Michigan.

"Ah, Aaron," said Aunt Louise, "'tis a pity you cannot write and let Maude know you're all right. For surely, she'll be worrying."

"I've been worrying over that myself, but how can I let her know without my father catching on?"

"It's true. If he were to find out, we'd have to send you back, or he might show up for you himself. There'd be nothing any of us could do but wave goodbye. Well," she concluded, "we'd best pray the angels let her know you're fine. That'll have to suffice, for I see no other way."

They threw a celebration that very weekend. Such a thing had not been done for me since my birthday parties when I was very young. I could not remember any of those. This one I would remember forever. The O'Sullivan house filled with people from the parish, including the priest, and the reveling lasted into the wee hours.

At this first party I met Kathleen's best friend, Susanna O'Connor—the most exquisite creature I had ever seen. Although her coloring was similar to Kathleen's, she had soft auburn curls, where Kathleen's hair was straight. Her features were delicate but large, her mouth curling upward at the corners as if ready to smile at the least provocation. Her slim body curved just so, gracefully bending into the loveliest of figures.

Smitten, I watched her the entire evening. My eyes sought her out even during the speeches in my honor, of which there were many, for a fair number at the party hailed from our area in Ireland. They all knew my father had stolen me, as there had been quite a search put out for us. It had been a sad thing, but on this day, all were happy that I was alive and well. As they spoke, my eyes wandered over the crowd until I found Susanna, who met my gaze and smiled or blushed numerous times. Too shy was I to speak to her directly, and then the evening was over.

The next day we went to Mass, where the priest acknowledged the miracle of my appearance on the O'Sullivans' doorstep and spoke of mourning circumstances that later turn out to be all right. It is something to consider, and I ponder it now, for didn't I agonize over things time and again during my life? In fact, after my demise, my period of mourning would seem unendurable.

How are we to rectify this mourning that, even when the situation seems bleakest and there appears to be no earthly way for things to "work out," still they have a way of doing so? It takes faith, of which I had little, and the patience to withstand such times. I had the latter, but without the faith, all is useless.

After Mass, Aunt Louise served a marvelous dinner at "our"

house. (I really began to feel I belonged there.) "This afternoon," she announced, "I'm going to write home and tell of your return, Aaron. But I'll be sure to warn against it getting back to your father."

"It's like he came back from the dead," laughed Kathleen's brother, repeating a theme we had heard constantly over the past few days.

"Tell them how you almost died from the fright of seeing him at the door, Mum," added Patty, her sister.

"Aye, we'll be telling the story for years to come," agreed Aunt Louise. She turned to Kathleen. "What will you be doing this afternoon, Kathleen?"

"Well," she answered, glancing sidelong at me, "it's a lovely day. I think Aaron and I should go for a little walk and visit Susanna." This idea had popped into my head the night before. I was helpless to know how to make it happen, but Kathleen had just solved the problem.

"Wonderful!" agreed Uncle Sean. Of medium build and thinning brownish hair, bespectacled and clean shaven, he was such a kind fellow. He went to his shop very early each day, and returned for a quick midday meal. We wouldn't see him again until early evening. He worked hard, yet always had energy for the family at night and on Sundays. Patient most of the time, he showed a slight frustration at the busyness of life. "What I would most enjoy," he'd say, "would be to pack it all up, go to the mountains and live off the land."

That afternoon, Kathleen and I strolled toward the O'Connor house.

"I saw the look in your eye last night, Mr. Aaron," Kathleen teased.

I felt the color rise to the roots of my hair.

"What you don't know is that I saw the same look in hers! Ha!" she hooted.

I looked at Kathleen with surprise. Not knowing Susanna, I'd had no idea that the lovely way she met my eyes was meant especially for me.

"And neither of you have the courage to talk to the other," she laughed, shaking her head. "Watched it all, I did, and I'll have none of that."

I glanced at her without understanding.

"If you want something, then you go after it, you do." When she saw what others wanted, she got it for them, too—a lovely quality at times that might be a problem at others.

"Ah, but Kathleen," I pleaded, "don't be making a fool of me."

"Fool? Hardly! Thinks you're the bee's knees, she does. Told me so herself today."

I had seen them giggling after Mass and wondered if it were about me, for didn't they keep looking my way from under their bonnets? Didn't like it, either, I'll have to admit. I thought they were making fun of the way I looked or something, but I was wrong. I must also admit that my eyes had again followed Susanna wherever she went, believing I was keeping cover. No doubt they'd noticed.

As we walked along the street on this beautiful Sunday afternoon in May, I glanced at my new friend. A rascal, Kathleen could put anyone up to anything. I had seen that. Didn't she have me doing her bidding now, and wasn't she playing matchmaker? But ask me if I minded. I was thrilled to have people care about my happiness. Looking back over it all later on in my experience— and I would have plenty of time for that—I saw that all through my childhood, with the exception a few important years, I always had someone to look out for me.

So now, here I was in the care of this lovely family—my own, in fact—and it was glorious. For the first time in my life, I felt truly safe. Even back in Ireland with Mummy to hide behind, my father had overlorded and overshadowed my existence. But free of his influence, I could truly be my own man, whoever that would be. I had been so stifled all my life that just being myself would be an adventure.

The first new thing I discovered about myself was that people found me interesting. Over and over, they asked about my experiences. I was finding again that being the center of attention was something I enjoyed, hearkening back to those days on the ship when I entertained the sailors. However, now I performed no stunts. Didn't need to. Telling the story and responding naturally to those around me was all that was necessary.

I looked at my cousin Kathleen with admiration for the fine bravado she displayed. She was a tough one. You could tell from the way she behaved with those around her. She loved to laugh, and would not listen to things that might pull her down. Mention my mother, and she regaled us with wonderful memories about her in Ireland. She would not recount Mummy's days of depression, her time spent in bed, unable to move even with my siblings to care for. No, Kathleen's eyes sparkled as she recalled some little tidbit my mother confided about my brothers or sisters, and I warmed to these stories of how Mummy loved us all so much.

Indeed, weren't Kathleen's eyes sparkling now as we covered the last block on our walk? "This is it!" she said, as we turned up the sidewalk to a white clapboard house surrounded by gardens and a white picket fence. She skipped to the door and rang the bell twice. Stepping back, she smiled down at her hands, then up at me, having a rollicking good time.

Susanna's father greeted us. "Good afternoon to the both of you!" He stepped back and held open the screen door. "Come in! Come in!" Then, "Susanna, your visitors have arrived."

Out from the back hallway came Mrs. O'Connor, a cheerful, homey person with green Irish eyes and red hair pulled into a knot that would not contain itself, wisps falling around her face and neck. "Oh, there you are Kathleen! And how nice to have *you* visit us, Aaron!" She wiped her hands on an apron tied around her mid-section, kissed Kathleen on the cheek, then turned to me and did the same.

Once again my color rose. I simply wasn't used to being around affectionate women. Maudie's kiss was the only one I had received from the age of four until just this past week. It was a little much to get used to overnight!

Then came Susanna down the stairs, so light on her feet I doubt they touched the steps. This time, it was a hug for Kathleen and a hand for me, thank the Lord. I took it in mine, inclining my head to her curtsy as our eyes locked.

It was to be the first of many such visits.

9

LESSONS
Boston, 1904

End of spring meant the end of the school year. Parochial schools were very good, and all the parish children attended. Though the issue as to whether I should also attend had not yet come up, it would not be long before it did, and I was not sure how to deal with it. I could read simple books, even some of Kathleen's and Susanna's, but when I saw their textbooks, journals and notebooks, it was plain as day that my writing and reading skills were lacking. Maudie had tried her best to catch me up before I ventured to Boston, but even at our accelerated rate, we had begun far too late. My new friends were far beyond me in their lessons. For a fact, I wasn't ready for high school.

Susanna, Kathleen and I enjoyed a lovely summer together. Able to shake off the younger siblings almost every day, we explored the waterfront and beaches. Many an hour we spent at the park just a few blocks from our home, where we talked about everything in life.

Kathleen doted on me. So funny was she in guessing what I wanted to do, or what I needed. Susanna and I got along famously.

And how thrilled Kathleen was for the two of us. She never became jealous of Susanna's attentions toward me, although there were times when Susanna would have wanted it to be just the two of us together, and I would have enjoyed that immensely. But we were young, and it was probably good that Kathleen was along. Without her, I'm afraid Susanna and I might have become more involved. We were not quite ready for that, although you couldn't have told me such a thing at the time. I was head-over-heels in love with Susanna.

Still am.

It had been idyllic, but August was upon us. With everyone thinking about the coming school year, I had to face this next step in my life, whatever it would be.

One afternoon, I was up in the garret having a rest, wondering if I should simply take a job instead of going to school, when I heard voices through the back window from the yard below. Aunt Louise and Mrs. O'Connor talked together as they took tea. I heard the words "he," "school," and "education" every once in a while. Reluctantly, I got up and descended the stairs, thinking that if there were to be a conversation about me, I would like to be in on it.

I walked out into the shaded yard and the ladies greeted me with pleasure.

"Why, there you are, dear," Aunt Louise said. "Did you have a good rest?"

Mrs. O'Connor looked up with a smile as she tucked a wisp of hair away from her face. "How are you, Aaron?"

Giving me no time to answer, Aunt Louise started right in. "We were just talking about you, Aaron. What do you think you'd like to do this coming school year?"

Wasn't that just the question, then? I moved to a chair. "I'm not sure I know what I *can* do." It was truthful enough. All right, I decided, I might as well come out with the rest of it, so I took the plunge. "I know I'm not up to high school yet."

Neither lady seemed surprised.

"You know, Aaron, Mrs. O'Connor has an idea you just might want to consider." Looking me straight in the eye I could see where Kathleen got her directness.

I turned to Mrs. O'Connor. "What is it?"

"Well, there's a woman in our parish, Mrs. Harris—a good woman—who is widowed, her children grown and gone," she said. "Now, Mrs. Harris has little to live on but gives all her time and much of what she has to the charities at church. I've worked with her and know her well. She's a smart one, is Mrs. Harris."

Aunt Louise nodded in agreement. "We know the kind of work she can do, Aaron. She's led committees and done the book work—the accounting, you know—for others."

Mrs. O'Connor continued without missing a beat. "But even with all the church work she does, she's got plenty of alone time on her hands. Father O'Brien's asked us to call on her from time to time."

Having no idea where this was going, I simply listened.

"Aaron," said Aunt Louise, "we think that perhaps Mrs. Harris might be able to help with your education." She looked at Mrs. O'Connor, then both looked at me.

I hadn't anticipated this. If Mrs. Harris was as good as they said, there might not be a break in my education! I felt my burden lift. It would work out, after all. "Do you think she'll do it?" I asked, and they knew I was in.

Mrs. O'Connor spoke with Father O'Brien, who spoke with

Mrs. Harris, who then got back in touch with Aunt Louise. The following Sunday after Mass, she approached with Mrs. Harris as I chatted under a tree with Kathleen and Susanna. They stepped away, allowing us privacy.

"Lottie Harris, meet the newest member of our household, Aaron Burke," said Aunt Louise.

"Aaron, it is a pleasure to behold your fine face, not at a distance or across the aisle, but up close so I can see what you're made of."

I looked into her eyes and felt my own brim up. I don't know why, but it seemed that this woman would fill a spot in my heart and in my being that had been empty for ever so long. I tilted my face to the sky until the water in my eyes settled, then looked back into Mrs. Harris's, seeing for sure what I perceived a moment before. Here was a woman who would listen to my hopes and my fears, who would guide me and side with me when life was difficult. This was a woman I could lean on, a woman I could trust, a woman of great depth.

"Mrs. Harris." I could barely speak, cleared my throat and began again. "Mrs. Harris, I believe the pleasure is mine."

We made a plan for me to visit her from 2 to 4 p.m. on Tuesdays and Thursdays. She lived a bit away from our house, so I took to riding a bike. Having never ridden one, didn't Kathleen and Susanna make sport of me, running alongside teaching me to balance, laughing as they let go, screaming as I went down. Actually, it didn't take but an afternoon for me to get the hang of it. A bit wobbly at first, with the three-mile ride to Mrs. Harris's, I was an expert in no time.

I had decided that a job to defray my living expenses and Mrs. Harris's fee would be a good idea. Also, though I could never repay the O'Sullivan's for putting me up, I could help.

Uncle Sean had other ideas. "Ah, save it, boy. You'll need it to buy the girls ice cream cones every now and then, along with your other expenses, don't you think?" The man had a good heart. "Keep it for your future, Aaron," he said another time. A wise businessman himself, he advised, "You never know when you'll need it."

As good as this man was, from the time I left my father, it was the women in my life who became the greater influence. Oh, Uncle Sean and Mr. O'Connor would figure into it to be sure, but neither they nor any male friend or relative in my future would compare in significance to the women with whom I shared life's experiences. I'm sure this was due to my early years with my father, but it's also clear that, although the men were kind and not a threat, I craved closeness with the women. I must state that this inability to have friendships with other men made me more gruff and distant with them than I might have been otherwise.

Neither did I warm to children in any way. Perhaps it was because I never had a real childhood—playing with others the way most children did—but I could no longer relate to them. You would think that the lack of a childhood would make a person become more attracted to things childish or yearn to have children around, but this was not the case with me. Kathleen had two younger brothers and three sisters, and Susanna an even larger family, yet I do not speak of them, for they were of little consequence to me. Oh, I liked them, but it was the women I needed.

Interestingly, though the lack of a childhood produced an alienation to things childish, the lack of a mother had just the opposite effect. I cannot explain it, only tell it the way it is. And so I unconsciously focused on my need for the feminine touch.

Discovering Mrs. Harris's "house" (really a set of third-floor rooms in Boston's seedier wharf district), I tied up my bike—which was likely to be stolen if I didn't—took the stairs three at a time and knocked on the door.

She swung it open with a delighted cry as if I hadn't been expected. "Aaron! How grand to have you call on me today!" The woman made you feel important. She invited me to sit by the window at a little table flanked by two dilapidated upholstered chairs. Yet the sheer tied-back curtains gave the place a glow as did this woman herself, and as time went on I came to forget I was in the shabby part of town. Instead, we were up and away from the street, looking over rooftops and through the treetops to the sea beyond.

My first lessons did not last past the four o'clock limit, as neither of us wanted to keep the other from the rest of the day's schedule. It soon became apparent, however, that both of us enjoyed our visits exceedingly, and we ignored the moving hand on the clock as it swept past the twelve and moved down again toward the six.

In all kinds of weather we sat and talked for hours on end, many times going right up to suppertime. On those days, I would jump up, say a quick thank you and goodbye, run for my bike and be off in a moment.

Supper was served when Uncle Sean got home at seven. If "Papa" were late, the meal would wait, but the rest of us were not allowed to tarry. I found that out the first time one of the boys did not come in from playing outside in the summer. His place sat unattended and when we finished the meal, his dishes were cleared with the rest and nothing more was said. He did show up halfway through, all apologetic, but the rest of the family treated him silently, and he turned and left the room, going to bed on an empty stomach.

I always made sure to be home by six.

Mrs. Harris invariably wanted to know how I was getting along in my new life before we began my exercises. In those first visits, I only talked about experiences relating directly to my studies. Once she had a feeling for how things were going and what my immediate educational needs were, she had me pull out my daily journal. Here was more food for discussion, for I wrote down everything happening in my life. Sometimes, she assigned essays expanding on my ideas.

Expressing myself on paper unleashed my demons. I wrote out my observations of other people, the importance of the relationships I'd had in my life, the horrific experiences I had endured with my father. I wrote of the trip overseas and the ship that brought us here. I wrote of Maudie and our alliance. And I wrote about Mummy. How he could have taken me from her I'll never know, but that one event above any other colored the very fabric of my being, and I wrote about it. Oh, did I write. Cried I did as I scribbled, smearing the ink till it was indecipherable, yet the emotion of those pages was clear as day. That first great sadness left a mark unlike any other.

I went to see Mrs. Harris for three years. We had a jolly time, for I consumed knowledge in an effort to get up to speed with everyone else. While Susanna and Kathleen worked on projects their teachers assigned, I was busy with Mrs. Harris, learning at a ferocious pace. Little did I know that in some ways I was surpassing them in considerations about life itself.

While the girls and I grew in knowledge, intellect, wisdom and maturity, Mrs. Harris remained steadfast, never changing, always there.

✤   ✤   ✤

There came a time in my second year of lessons when Susanna and I were on the outs over an observation I made. She was always on me about the way I criticized people. I didn't see it as criticism. It was the truth.

"You'd better watch that neighbor of yours," I remarked one day as we sat in the yard. The man next door had been looking our way more often than not as he pruned his bushes. "He's a little too interested in what we do, if you're asking me."

"Aaron, how can you say that?"

"Well, look at him nosing over this way, watching you, listening to us."

She looked over, but the man moved in the other direction. (Heard what I said, didn't he?)

"He's just pruning his bushes."

"Susanna, you want to believe people are good, but sometimes they have ulterior motives. What he's interested in is none of his business."

"Oh, Aaron! I've known Mr. Benson my whole life. He's not like that at all!" She jumped up and headed for the house in a huff. "Sometimes, you sound like a mean old man!"

I supposed I did at that, even if I did speak the truth. Old men usually do. I guessed I was an old seventeen.

Susanna needed a break from my presence and would not agree to be with me at all. Kathleen, tried to intercede, but Susanna would not have it, and I was bereft. Ah, it hurt to be without my best friend.

On these occasions, my visits with Mrs. Harris consisted simply of talks about life. Oh, she had heard and read my opinions of people in general, remarking on how "interesting" they were. I had taken her comments to be positive, but now these same observations were getting me in hot water. What was I to do, not share my thoughts with my loved one? How could one hold in what one was?

"Ah, Aaron," she sighed one afternoon as we sipped tea by the window, "you've learned to hold yourself in when you don't trust a person, have you not?"

I looked down at my reflection as it shimmered on the dark surface inside the cup. "I did when I lived with my father, but that's different. If you let someone you don't trust know how you feel, you're letting yourself in for it."

"The same goes with those you love, Aaron. You know they love and accept you as a person. That doesn't mean they have to agree with you on everything. If you love Susanna for who she is, don't force your views on her. Let her be herself."

After a life of being wrong, I so wanted others to believe in me, I would press to the limit for them to see I was right. "So if I share ideas I know Susanna won't agree with, I should allow her to respond in her own way." Did I want to bully her into seeing everything the way I did? Didn't I love her *because* of the way she was already, whether we agreed on everything or not?

"Don't you want a more tranquil relationship that fulfills you both?"

Susanna and I soon made amends, and after that I tried to follow my teacher's advice. Now when Susanna drew back at one of my snide remarks, I looked at my tendency to do so and saw that I was not on such a high pedestal myself. Who was I to judge others, anyway? True, I did perceive things about people, could see right through some of them in fact—a gift that could bring great wisdom. But if I wasted it by overly criticizing instead of using it to keep away from those who were more unsavory, then I was a fool after all.

I loved my visits with Mrs. Harris. Having been in her home many times, I was comfortable examining her books, her figurines, and her collections as she prepared tea. Often, religious objects on a corner table caught my eye. I finally asked about them.

"Oh, those belonged to my parents."

I examined a candelabrum, an engraved goblet, books filled with strange print. "What language is this?" I asked, rifling through one of them.

"That's Hebrew, Aaron. I'm Jewish."

"But you're Catholic."

"My husband's family was Catholic. The Church wouldn't let us marry unless I converted, so I did," she said. "Now that he's gone, I bring out the candles on Friday night and observe the Sabbath on Saturdays."

So that was why our visits were on Tuesdays and Thursdays instead of on weekends. Here I had been visiting Mrs. Harris twice a week for an entire year; we'd poured our hearts out to each other, and I hadn't known this about her. In fact, I had never met anyone before who was Jewish. At least, I didn't know it, if they were.

I had more questions. "But still you come to Mass."

"That church means a great deal to me. My friends are there, my children were baptized there, I was married there, and Mr. Harris is buried there. Many celebrations of life and death in my family happened in that church."

I picked up the candelabrum to study it, listening, thinking.

"Most of all, Aaron, the Father is present wherever we are. It doesn't matter if we're Catholic or Protestant or Jewish, don't you see? Any road we take to stay in touch with Him is good as long as we don't hold ourselves above others who do the same in their own way. That is where the evil comes into religion. Besides, if our way is the only way, how can we grow? Even at the highest spiritual levels, there is room to grow.

"Have you not learned that yourself, in your dealings with Susanna? If she disagrees with you, listen to her. You might learn something. It's the same with spiritual matters. If someone has something different to say, listen. A kernel of truth could germinate and grow to be a glorious, flowering tree.

"Saddest of all is that the very thing which should bring us the greatest peace and tranquility—the love of the Father above—produces the greatest conflict and wars. More evil has been done in the name of religion than any other, and all because people think their way is the only way. Ah, Aaron. Sometimes the world is topsy-turvy."

I looked at her. To be able to give up her religion, yet hold onto who she was, coming back full circle one day —what a wondrous thing.

No conflicts existed in her. I wondered why. "Mrs. Harris, you seem so peaceful. Don't you conflict inside over anything?"

"Aaron, the most important thing of all is to find inner peace. If we are confused about something, it shows up in our daily dealings. How can we live a clear life if we're muddled up inside? And if everyone were muddled, what kind of world would it be?

"No, if I'm disturbed over something, I get quiet inside, ask for guidance and then go on with my day."

"What happens then?"

"Sometime later, I'll have a new way of seeing it, and I'm no longer confused. Then I give thanks and go on. You see, people usually pray about problems when life is already going wrong. But when I pray, I get to my own discord and ask for clarity before it has a chance to develop. If something troubles me, I pray. If I am not sure how to think about something, I pray over it. Soon, a wiser, larger way of looking at the situation presents itself.

"I did that when I met Mr. Harris and learned he was Catholic. Knew right away what it would do to my parents to see me convert. I had to work out in my own mind what was the best thing to do, right then. Disagreements still came, but at least I knew where I stood, and that made for fewer arguments because I just knew."

I thought I saw a contradiction. "But weren't you holding your own opinions above those of others?"

"Well," she smiled, "there is a delicate balance to keep when one 'knows' inside. We have to remember that we only know for ourselves. What is right for me might not be true and right for you. Some people say that what is right for one is right for all, but that's what leads us down the path to war, you know. Other people are going to see it differently, and there we go again. We really only know for ourselves, Aaron."

"I can see why you are so peaceful and have room in your heart for so many people," I said. "You find truth for yourself and let others find theirs." I thought a moment. "I suppose when you're talking with someone you offer your opinion if they're listening, and if not, you let it go because they're struggling, too."

"And I never see them as wrong, Aaron. Once we get into right and wrong, it's all over. No, what's right for me is right only for me, and that's all. A person knows, and it is not for others to question."

That brought up another point. "Mrs. Harris, what happens when they try to get *you* to see things *their* way?"

"I always listen." Of course. She'd just said that. "None of us is perfect, and there's always more to learn. Even the poor beggar on the street has learned a thing or two from life." I nodded at the sense of it. "You'll find wisdom wherever you go if you always listen." She brightened. "And the other person appreciates it so. You know, most people have their minds made up and don't want to hear. God forbid someone should shake their foundation." Her eyes softened as she took my hand in hers. "But find someone who will listen to you, and it's as if Heaven has opened its Gates."

We sat back down by the window. "Mrs. Harris," I said, "you're incredible."

After fifteen years of difficulty, to be loved by such people as the O'Sullivans, the O'Connors and Mrs. Harris, as well as being embraced by the entire congregation at St. Mary's, was heaven. I truly felt as if I had been adopted—so much so that instead of a middle name which no one would remember, I adopted my mother's maiden name of O'Malley. Aaron O'Malley Burke I was now, a man with family who loved him.

My seventeenth birthday came and went. Aunt Louise actually knew the date, April the third, and there were grand parties. The Irish love to celebrate life, and celebrate we did. Whenever friends had a special event, they celebrated. Births, baptisms, weddings, baby and wedding showers beforehand for the ladies, graduations, new jobs, retirements, and all of the holidays were cause to drop everything and have a special day.

By the time of my eighteenth birthday, Susanna and Kathleen were ready to graduate from high school. I, having studied with Mrs. Harris for nearly three years, had almost caught up with them, amazingly enough. In fact, what Mrs. Harris taught me about life was of far greater value than anything one could get in a school, although we didn't know that then.

One blowy Thursday in late March, on my way to see my teacher, I rounded the corner of her building and saw a group of people gathered near an ambulance and paddy. My heart clenched, then began to pound. I raced up, threw down my bike, and pushed my way through the crowd.

A policeman blocked me with his arm. "Here, here now."

They had her on a stretcher. Covered with bruises and cuts she was, her clothes torn, a shoe missing. She looked very bad, did Mrs. Harris. I didn't know whether she was dead or alive.

I had to get to her. "But it's Mrs. Harris! She's family!"

"Mrs. Harris, is it? And if she's family, why do you call her 'Mrs.'? Tell me that now."

"She's *like* family. Please let me go to her."

She was not dead after all, for I heard her voice call my name. It was very weak indeed. The policeman heard it, too, and let me go to her side as they loaded her into the ambulance.

"Mrs. Harris!"

"Aaron." She looked terrible and so, so sad.

The man lifting her into the vehicle said, "You can come, if you like." I climbed in. They secured the stretcher onto its ledges, closed the back doors, and the driver started through the maze of people.

I took her hand. How cold it was. "Oh, Mrs. Harris, whatever happened?"

She spoke in fits and starts. "They. . . didn't like me."

"Who didn't like you?"

A big breath. A weaker voice. "Never did."

I couldn't imagine anyone not liking her, and looked to the driver.

"Three youths accosted her," he said.

My eyes widening, I looked back at her. "What were you doing when they attacked you?"

"Market," she said and closed her eyes again. She had been on her way home from the market in time for our visit, and three youths attacked her?

"But why didn't they like you?"

She could hardly speak. "Jew."

What? How did they know? And what difference could that make?

She must have sensed my questions. "Sabbath. Lighting..."

I didn't get it.

She answered a few minutes later. "...in the window," she finished, winced, then closed her eyes.

"She'd best rest now," said the aide.

They saw her lighting Sabbath candles and attacked her because she was different?

Scum! Idiots! I hated them!

I sat holding her hand as we rode through this squalid part of town.

She opened her eyes—now sharp, clear, focused. But her voice waned. "Aaron, don't." I lowered my ear to hear. "It will ruin you," she whispered.

I looked at her again, questioning.

Unable to answer, her eyes locked mine as she breathed with

great difficulty. It was a few minutes before she regained her breath. "Don't...hate...back." Her next words floated as if on a breeze passing through her. "It will...ruin...you."

Her breath left in a long sigh, and I watched the light leave her eyes. Still looking at me, they no longer saw. Just like that, she was gone.

Oh, no.

The aide reached to touch her.

My tears flew as I whirled on him. "What are you doing?"

He reached past me and closed her eyes.

"How dare you! She was just talking to me."

He said nothing.

I looked back at Mrs. Harris, her face turning gray. My gaze fell to her hand, unbruised, uncut, still in mine. Wouldn't at least a nail be broken?

Ah, Mrs. Harris, Mrs. Harris. You never lifted a finger to defend yourself, did you?

For the life of me, I could not let go of her hand.

❖   ❖   ❖

The funeral was the next day—Friday—immediate in the Jewish way, for Saturday would have been her Sabbath, and the church would not have it on theirs. There was no viewing, of course, for she was a wreck.

I remember little of this funeral; no happy stories were in it for me. Anything anyone said about her goodness made it worse— made me angry, in fact. I knew this woman better than any of them, didn't I? Hadn't we shared the stories of our entire lives with each other, all of our secrets? It never occurred to me that she had done the same with many of these folks. Shattered, I spoke to no one.

After the ceremony, I climbed to my room in the loft and looked across the rooftops and treetops toward Mrs. Harris's place. The family kept a respectful distance, since I was rather ugly to be around.

A few days later, I ventured out to nearby bars and pubs. They let me in now, just shy of eighteen. I became a nasty drunk, imagining slights and starting fights, getting kicked from one tavern to another, coming home later and later, until one night when I didn't come home at all.

Flat out I was, waking under a bench outside a pub on the outskirts of town. I neither remembered going into this bar nor my trip out of it, but there I was. Sitting up, I endeavored to gather my senses. I looked around, thinking it nighttime still, but no, it was bright all about.

Came to me plain as day she did, not dead after all.

"Why Mrs. Harris," I said. "Whatever are you doing here?"

She smiled. "Aaron, my boy. What are *you* doing here?"

"But I thought you were . . ."

"Aaron, you mustn't do this to yourself."

I looked down, ashamed.

"It was my time to go, don't you see? Much better to make a point of it when you die than not."

I had no idea what she meant. *Make a point of what?*

"Aaron, I would have gone soon enough. Those boys are in jail, where they belong, because of what they did. Do you think it's the first time they bothered me and everyone else who's a tad different?"

I sat, dumb.

"Those boys had been harassing people for a long time. Better to put them behind bars for their lives when mine is over than leave them to badger others," and she vanished into thin air.

And I, incapable even of wondering where she went, fell back to a deep sleep.

I awoke at dawn with an enormous ache in my head. My eyes were blurry and my stomach upside down, but my mind was clear, and as I sat up again outside that bar, it was unmistakable to me that she had stood right by that tree. I stumbled over to it, searching for a sign of her. Seeing none, I squinted at the sky, determining that it must be nearly seven in the morning, and started for home.

When the door opened, there was Aunt Louise, concern and kindness etched upon her face. I felt my own crumple and started to cry. She caught me in her arms and somehow managed to close the door.

"Ah, now Aaron," she whispered.

I sobbed.

"Now, now. You'll be healing, I believe."

She led me into the parlor and sat me down. Held me she did, and I let it all out, all the anger and fear and hurt I had felt for ever so long, in a fit of crying such as I had never known.

After that, I began to recover and allowed the family to subdue my pain in any manner they were willing. My feelings of unworthiness came out in countless ways, all of them shoved aside by these admirable people. Aunt Louise made my favorite meals. She brought me tea as I sat staring into nothingness, deep in thought. Kathleen would come over, sit on the arm of the chair and put her arm across my shoulder. We would sit for a while; then she would leave me to think or suggest something like a walk to the park.

Gradually, I was able to go out without being angry at the "ways of the world." For in truth, I had been as bad as any, targeting this person or that with my own anger and hatred. And wasn't that just the lesson Mrs. Harris had tried to teach me? What a poor student I was. Over and over I caught myself seeing some fault in another and responding with loathing, but now I was aware of it. Children were cruel to each other, and I abhorred their cruelty, then looked at my abhorrence. I overheard passersby make boorish remarks and reacted with revulsion, then smiled. Who did I think I was, anyway? What made me better than them?

Mrs. Harris's lessons brought me to look at myself time and again. I thought about the talk we had about allowing Susanna to be her own self, but that was a piece of cake compared to looking at these people and allowing them to be the nincompoops they were. Ah, there I went again. I saw my own hypocrisy and hated it, then laughed.

As I stood back and looked at myself the way I had always viewed others, I beheld everything I ever despised.

I O

LOVE
Boston, 1907

It seemed I was doomed to be judgmental and angry until Susanna came to visit one day, and the two of us went for a stroll in the park. We walked slowly, looking around us, pointing this or that out to each other. I began to notice the beauty of the day. We stopped and sat on a bench. We were comfortable enough, but I needed her to be closer and reached my arm around her shoulder, pulling her to me. She allowed herself to be drawn in right next to me. For a long time we sat letting the closeness settle in, until finally I spoke.

"Ah, Susanna."

She watched the children play across the field as she swung her legs over the grass, her feet brushing the blades, and listened.

"I have to apologize."

She looked down, still silent.

"I've been so angry and terrible to be around."

"Aaron," she murmured, an acknowledgement that I had apologized enough.

"I can't make sense of it," I continued.

"I know."

"Mrs. Harris was so wonderful. Why couldn't they see that? She never hurt anyone."

"It's true."

In my mind, a picture unfolded of Mrs. Harris and me sipping tea at her front window. "I learned so much more from her than just reading and writing. She was the wisest person I've ever known, and now she's gone." The picture in my head vanished.

Susanna turned to me, my arm still around her. "But Aaron." Her lips were ever so near. "That is her legacy to you. Her wisdom."

How true. Mrs. Harris had little to pass on by way of physical wealth, but what she had given me was worth worlds more than gold and diamonds.

Ah, but where is it now? I wondered.

Reminiscing, I said, "She was clear, never confused. I'd come to her so perplexed—like I am now—and she'd turn me right around."

"Well," said Susanna, an idea building inside her, "if you were with her today, befuddled like you are," she smiled, teasing, then turned serious again, "what would she say?"

I paused. "I don't know. It's all gone. I can't figure anything out without her."

"Well, how did *she* stay so clear?"

And then I remembered. "She said that when something bothered her, she got quiet and asked for help in straightening it out inside herself."

We sat for a long time, looking at the trees, the flowers, the clouds above while I had a little inner conversation asking to be clear and able to straighten things out. Even with everything that had happened in my life, I had never truly prayed for myself, and it felt good.

I sighed and turned to Susanna. "Thank you."

She looked at me, surprised. "For what?"

"For helping me understand what to do."

She was thoughtful for a moment. "You're welcome, Aaron." She smiled her beautiful smile, her face so close to mine. "You're welcome."

And I kissed her. Right there in the park, in broad daylight, for anyone to see. She didn't pull back or act embarrassed. Then we looked at each other.

The softest smile played around her mouth. "I want to always be able to help you."

They say that when one door closes, another opens. My relationship with Susanna would blossom as I healed from the loss of my wonderful teacher. It wasn't that Susanna could ever replace Mrs. Harris or that our relationships were even alike; but she did become a confidante, and I shared my doubts and problems with her just as I had with my mentor. This I desperately needed, for otherwise I felt shut out from people, just as I had been as a small boy.

I never wanted to be like that again.

❖   ❖   ❖

I formally courted Susanna for nearly two years. We were on our way to a life of our own yet not quite ready to take on its responsibilities. She attended finishing school, and I had to figure out how to manage financially once we were married. I moved up to chief manager at the hardware store with four employees under me. Though happy with my progress, I could see the day fast approaching when I would outgrow this business.

In my nineteenth year, Susanna and I looked forward to nuptials. The prospect of living with her parents the first few years of our marriage wasn't necessarily to our liking but made things more economical. Unfortunately, it wasn't to work out as we expected.

The call came in the form of a wire two months before the scheduled wedding.

FATHER NOT IN GOOD HEALTH STOP CANNOT WORK FARM STOP NEEDS HELP OR SELL STOP JEREMY FOUND YOU STOP WHAT TO DO STOP MAUDIE

I wrote back telling her to sell, but it wasn't as easy as that.

FATHER NOT GOOD STOP CANNOT SELL BY HIMSELF STOP PLEASE COME STOP MAUDIE

Susanna said, "We must go."

"But the wedding . . ." I began.

"She needs us now," she replied.

Of course, the conversation should have been reversed. I should have been the one insisting we return, but I didn't want to go back. I never wanted to see him again, yet I owed Maudie. It was the right thing to do.

We married the week after my birthday. Susanna and I waltzed until dawn. Bittersweet was the occasion, for though I had my darling, we would be leaving family and friends. Two days later, we boarded the train that would take us to the place in northern

Michigan I had hoped I would never see again. This time, the railroad took us all the way to Empire, just a few miles south of the farm. The logging business was still in full swing, and a little branch of the railroad ended there at the docks.

Although I was downhearted most of the trip, the strange thing was that as we went farther north, Susanna became increasingly amazed at the magnificence of the land. "It's so beautiful, Aaron."

It was as if I were seeing it for the first time. A child when we originally came here, never do I remember enjoying Michigan scenery. Yet with Susanna at my side, northern Michigan was beautiful. Blue lakes with pine-fringed coasts spotted the countryside. Rich, loamy farmland rolled across meadows. Rivers and streams wound through forests bursting with wildlife. Early spring flowers bloomed, birds sang, and every once in a while, deer grazed at forest's edge.

I gazed upon the face of my beloved. "You," I said.

She looked at me, eyebrows raised.

"You're the reason."

"For what? What have I done now?" The tease of a pout played on her face, excruciatingly beautiful.

"Your presence makes this place as beautiful as you are."

"Pish-posh. It was this way before I was ever born. You're the one who's different."

I thought about that. I had learned a lot about myself over the last five years. I was good at some things—that I knew now. Maudie had told me I was good with letters and numbers, but we hadn't really put it to the test until I left. Mrs. Harris and our family and friends had shown me I was acceptable, which was a lot more than I had ever felt about myself while living here. Except, of course, with Maudie. She accepted me from the moment she saw me, but I had attributed it more to her way than what she saw in me.

Ah, Maudie. How had she held up over these last few years? Was she as spry as she had been when I left, or had my father worn her down, too? I had often thought about her during my time in Boston. How had she fared?

I saw her before we were even off the train. You couldn't miss that bonnet and large frame. I would have recognized her any-where. "Maudie!" I shouted over the locomotive's clamor as we made our way to where she stood.

"Ronie!"

I embraced her and then stepped back. It had been hard, indeed. Gray she was—not just her hair but her entire demeanor. Where was the life that had been in her when she sent me on my way? And those lines around her eyes and mouth hadn't been there when I left, had they? *Oh, Maudie,* I thought. *What has he done to you?*

She'd also been appraising me. "You've done well, my boy," she said with a proud smile.

I pulled Susanna forward by the elbow. "Maudie, meet Susanna, my wife." Now this was a surprise. I had wired nothing about Susanna, simply the logistics of my return.

I believe Maudie had thought Susanna a cousin of some sort. "What? Your wife?" She looked at me in astonishment, then at Susanna. "Really?" she asked Susanna, who nodded, her smiling eyes alight, and then the fire came back into Maudie's, too.

"Susanna, this is Maudie."

"I'm so pleased to meet you, Maudie," Susanna said, extend-ing her gloved hand.

Maudie gave Susanna a big hug. "Pleased ain't the word for it!

You're just the thing!" she cried and started laughing and laughing. "God has a way, doesn't He, Ronie?"

I had to agree.

We loaded our bags in the buggy and started for the farm.

Maudie filled us in. "You're father hasn't been himself since you left," she said, serious now.

The old guilt found its way into my heart. I'd done something wrong again. It was my fault he wasn't well.

Unaware, Maudie continued. "He was mighty exasperated when he came in that first day to find you had disappeared. We looked all through town, asking this person and that. No one had seen you, of course. I did my part in acting innocent, and I don't think he ever suspected what I did. He finally accepted you were gone for good when you didn't come back that first winter.

"Had a hard time farming alone, but managed to put in a decent crop and got some of those boys from town you don't think much of to help him out at harvest time. Come the next spring, he wasn't quite up to farming the entire field, so he rented off a third of it. The following year he rented off a little more and the past two years he hasn't farmed at all.

"Been coughing up a spell this past winter and doesn't seem to be able to get himself out of bed lately, though he wouldn't hear of not coming back out to the farm this spring." She paused. "I think he's going down, Aaron, I really do. You'll see it when you come in.

"He doesn't know you're coming, so you'll have to act like this was unplanned. We'll say you wired me yesterday, and I wanted it to be a nice surprise for him. He thinks I've just gone into the grocery."

We rode in silence for a while. My mind went over just how

much suffering my leaving had caused.

She must have sensed my thoughts. "Ain't no way I'd a done it different," she said. "You would have died here living with him, no doubt about it. I knew the anger and frustration you showed at those boys in town was misplaced from what you felt toward your papa. All that would have happened to you is work, work, work and never fitting in with anyone. I had to get you away from here so you could see what you were made of. A fine thing, too, I must say." She nodded and smiled at Susanna riding next to her in the front of the buggy.

The gentle wind fluttered our hair as we rode along on this unseasonably warm April day. I sat behind looking at the familiar scenery.

Susanna looked back at me, pleased; but when she saw my face, concern clouded hers. "Aaron, don't," she said.

"If I hadn't gone, he'd be okay."

"What?!!" cried Maudie, turning halfway around to see my miserable face. "Here, now, we'll have none of that! What have I been doing, slaving away all these years, the only joy in it knowing I did some good for you, getting you out of here so you could find yourself?" She was angry now. "And you'll throw all that away because he's in poor health? Because if you make yourself to blame, then I might as well, too, for you know whose idea it was in the first place, my dear man! Sorry I am to have to call you back is all I can say, but you had to see for yourself what was happening."

I don't think she had ever called me a man before. And I was now, wasn't I? No longer his boy, his slave, I was my own person, able to make decisions on my own regardless of him. And I had Maudie to thank for it. If it hadn't been for her, I wouldn't even have Susanna.

Another thing. Father had brought this on himself by forcing me to come with him to America in the first place.

I had to think from this perspective for Maudie and Susanna—and for myself. Etching these thoughts into my heart, I bucked up for what was to come.

"I'm sorry, Maudie," I said. "It's hard not to get caught up into my old ways of thinking."

It became clear as we approached that things had fallen into severe disrepair. Maudie spoke up. "The farm says it all." She was right about that. It looked terrible. Maudie had done her best, but fences had fallen apart, the door to the barn hung from one hinge, and a stable window had broken. Tools lay all over the place. I wondered if they had been out all winter. Sure looked like it. The house needed painting, the roof needed shingles, and the front step had broken down. What a mess! I looked at Susanna, who was as appalled as I.

We got out of the buggy and picked a path up the broken steps, but our spirits lifted as we entered. Maudie had a cheerful way of keeping house, though a coat of paint wouldn't hurt in here either. Things were more worn, but otherwise, it looked pretty much the same inside as when I left.

"Why, it's lovely," uttered Susanna.

"He's in his room," said Maudie. His room? And where was Maudie's? "Here's your room, Ronie. I didn't know you were bringing a lady, so I don't have extra towels out. I'll get them." She bustled off as Susanna and I stood in the doorway to my room.

It was so small. I remembered when we added this room after my father and Maudie had married. Such a happy time for me. Having Maudie in our lives had made a difference, but never had

I dreamed I could be as happy as I was now with Susanna, even in this horrible man's house.

"Well," said Susanna, taking charge, "let's bring in our things and settle them." She looked up at me and smiled. "It will be all right. You'll see."

I brought in our bags and began to unpack but found myself drawn away.

I had to see him. Alone.

His door was closed. Turning the latch, I stepped into the darkened bedroom. An awful stench that can only be described as decay hit me. I wasn't sure of the exact cause, but it was evident he was dying. He lay under the covers, his chest working hard. Each breath crackled with what lay inside killing him. I cannot say he looked smaller to me, just different. Never would I have recognized this to be the man who ruled my existence all those years. His hair had turned gray, though I doubt he was fifty. (I really didn't know his age.) A veneer of sweat coated his yellowed face. His eyes closed, he breathed with his mouth open. He was not aware of my presence.

I moved closer.

His eyes flew open. The old venom flashed behind them and crashed into the pit of my stomach.

"What are *you* doing here?"

Terrified, I wanted to get out. I took a deep breath instead. "I've come for a visit."

"Finally, eh?" His laugh turned into a wracking cough.

Maudie ran in and made her way around to the other side of the bed. "Look who's come to see us, Edward!" Her brightness did little to assuage the tone of our conversation.

"Took your own sweet time, didn't you, boy?" I was a boy

again. His boy, his servant. He looked at the way I was dressed. "Never sent me any of that green stuff you've obviously gotten your hands on either." His voice rasped over my nerves. "Where'd you finally end up then, *if* I may ask?" He shot me a look so full of hatred, it took my breath away.

Shocked, I stepped back, separating myself from the old emotions connected to him and began to see him in a different way. Who did this person think he was to take me from my own mother, to keep me from an education, to impose himself on me now or ever again? How did I survive all those years living with this?

Drawing myself up as tall as I could, I thrust out my chest. "I went to find my mother's people." Firm was my voice; firm, my being. This man was pitiful. He was not to be bowed down to. He was nothing to me.

Irritation curled the edge of his voice. "Now, where would you do that?"

"I found them in Boston. They took me in, found me a good job and gave me an education—did for me what you never did. And—they loved me." I walked out.

"You come back here, boy," he yelled, then succumbed to another fit of coughing.

I would not submit to the demons within him nor within me that called for subservience. I was through with that. A man I was now. I would not be his "boy" again. Ever.

Maudie tried to subdue him, but he yelled and ranted and raved until his cough made it impossible to say another word. He hacked away in a fit for a long time, then settled down and was quiet.

Shaking, I went back to our room and sat in the chair by the bed while Susanna put our things away. I got up and closed the door. "I don't know why we came here," I said.

She knelt in front of me, one hand on my knee. "We came to help Maudie. Aaron, things will work out. And we can leave as soon as you wish."

"That man had me in his grips for a minute. I'll never let it happen again!"

"That's right. You never have to do that again. Now," she said, efficient as she stood and moved back to the open suitcase, "let's put these away and get out of these fancy clothes and into something we can work in so I can go out and help Maudie, shall we?" She looked up from the shirt she was refolding and gave me the most delicious smile.

Everything else melted away and became nothing. How ephemeral it all is!

In the following days, Maudie took care of my father while Susanna cared for the house. I, wanting to be as far from him as possible, worked outside on the land, which had been left fallow. I had only a few weeks to get it ready for planting, but before I could do that, I had to mend tools, order seed, and see to the animals, which had been sorely overlooked. There was much to do, and I kept right at it, avoiding further contact with my father.

I never did see him again. Oh, I heard him coughing and ordering Maudie around. There was little one could do to escape what was happening under that small roof. I even heard him ask about Susanna and me. But I never went into his room nor could he come out. Maudie tried to reason with me when it became obvious he would not make it. But as he became weaker, my resolve became stronger.

We stayed up the night he died. Susanna and I, in the living room, noted the increasingly labored breathing as the evening progressed. Maudie stayed with him. We knew he was gone from the sudden quiet in his room. After a bit, Maudie came to the door and nodded.

I looked down, then back up to her and said, "Come here, Maudie," patting the space on the loveseat next to me. Susanna had curled up in the overstuffed chair across from us. Maudie sat down and heaved a big sigh. There was not much to say about his going except that it was over. "Thank you, Maudie, for taking care of him," I said. "I couldn't have done it."

She reached over and patted my hand. "There, there. That's quite all right, Aaron. It's been hard for you just being under the same roof with him." She looked at Susanna. "And you, Missy. I have to thank you from the bottom of my heart for taking over the household like you did."

Susanna smiled her winsome little smile. Loving to see the corners of her lips curl up before the rest of her mouth followed, I smiled inside. "Oh, Maudie, you're welcome," she said. "You couldn't do all that by yourself for much longer."

"Well, you came just at the right time, I'll say."

"I'm glad you called for us, Maudie," Susanna said, and I studied her a second time. Susanna had worked hard to keep the house up and prepare meals, quite a different life than what she had been used to back in Boston—so much more work involved. But she never complained and seemed happy to do it. "It made me feel good to do something really helpful."

Ah, I thought. *She needs to feel essential.* In Boston, I had caught her lamenting her uselessness. Constantly talking about doing something meaningful in life, she had been at a loss over what she might contribute, feeling she had few talents. For me, just watching her being who she was lit up my day. But it wasn't enough for her, and she hushed me whenever I voiced my feelings about her worthiness. Now I understood why she hadn't complained over this hard work. Happy to be of use, these last few weeks provided her with a cause. I sat back on the loveseat and sighed. I already loved her so much. Knowing how she felt, I appreciated her even more.

The three of us soaked in the silence, letting death's finality sink in, none of us quite ready to resume activity. But soon, bleary-eyed, we kissed each other goodnight and slept well for the first time in weeks.

❖ ❖ ❖

The funeral was large for that town, mainly because everyone loved Maudie. They turned out for miles around in a grand procession to the cemetery. We all went back to her house afterward. She and Susanna had opened it up, freshening it for the wake. Guests poured in with all kinds of food inside and libation for the men outside.

It was a bit of a celebration as funerals ought to be. This time it did not celebrate the deceased's life, but the freedom his passing brought to the rest of us. Enough of the townspeople had heard his rantings through the walls that they had a small idea of what we went through in his lifetime. It also honored my return and marriage. Many of the folks had not yet seen me nor met Susanna, so there was plenty of joy to go around.

Maudie took her old name of Whitcomb back. Her first marriage had been such a happy one, she wanted to identify with him rather than my father. Can't blame her for that.

She wanted to live in her own house now, too. "It's only

right," she said one night at the farmhouse. "I still have my little place in town. You have Susanna now, Aaron, and you'll be building a family."

"You'll be all right alone, Maudie?" I asked.

She laughed. "Better than all right. Besides, I won't be alone much. My friends will be visiting, you know."

After Maudie had gone home, Susanna and I celebrated our first night alone with a special supper. We ate using our wedding silver, a lace tablecloth and flowers on the table. I asked Susanna if she was ready to return to Boston.

"Aaron, it's so pretty here." She glowed. "The farm's beautiful, and the town is so quaint, and with the beaches and lakes and rivers all around us, it's perfect for bringing up a family."

"Oh, I don't know. Winters here are fierce, Susanna, and farming life isn't easy."

She stuck out her lower lip in a false pout—so cute. "Don't I look strong enough to be a farming wife?"

That was it for me. Whatever she wanted she could have if I could give it to her.

"Just one thing," she added.

"And what would that one thing be?"

"We have to get a sailboat."

"A sailboat? Oh, I'm not a sailor, Susanna. Wouldn't know which end is front or rear."

"Please, Aaron!" She ran to my side and circled her arms around my neck. "The lakes are so lovely. Can you imagine being out in the middle of one on a balmy summer's day? Please!"

Done. "All right."

She squealed, jumping up and down. Pulling me up, she hugged me and turned me round and round. Singing a little tune,

she waltzed me through the house, ending the dance in our bedroom.

I, for one, was not sure about living in this place. With so
many memories tied to my father, I could hardly imagine a satis-
factory life here. But I had watched folks during the funeral and
saw how happy and hearty they all seemed. So now I thought, *Why
not?* For one thing, the crops were in. And in my frenzy to stay out
of the house during these last weeks, I had mended the fences and
replaced the broken windows. The animals were getting the nour-
ishment they had so desperately needed. I gave them plenty of
love and attention, taking the horses for rides with Susanna every
day. We explored places I had never been allowed to visit as a
boy—places I hadn't even known existed. Breathtaking vistas
unfolded as we topped each hill, and we'd stop to drink in the
magnificent splendor.

That summer, I did purchase a small sailing sloop, and we took
lessons. Once we were pronounced seaworthy, Susanna would
pack a lunch, and we'd sail far out on the bay, halfway to the
islands. More often than not, we lost the lunch as we came about
or when a gust of wind caught the sail, heeling the boat. Susanna
screamed and laughed, holding on.

One time we tipped completely over. That wasn't so funny. We
found it difficult to right the boat, much less stay afloat in our
heavy clothes. A sailor in a dinghy finally came out and rescued us.
After that, we wore lighter attire and sailed only in a steady wind.

The weather cooperated that year, and the crop was full.
Toward harvest we still had my savings from Boston along with
gift money from our wedding. We tucked it away, knowing the
harvest would be good, and it was.

We didn't do much socially outside of seeing Maudie from

time to time. Didn't need to. Susanna was enough for me. Besides, townspeople could be stuffy and gossipy, and I didn't want anything to spoil our life together.

That winter was the happiest time of my entire life. Susanna made a good home for us, repairing what she could, and I assisted at night mending broken chair legs and sanding down furniture she wished to refinish. Maudie had left us her old furnishings as a wedding present, so our house was complete from the outset. We bleached out Father's room and made it into a guestroom, should anyone ever care to visit. No one did, and that didn't bother us.

Susanna and I were so cozy in the farmhouse. I made sure it was ready for the cold weather, insulating and fixing any loose boards or windows. We put shutters on for the storms and frigid times, keeping ourselves warm by the fire in the house and in our love. Susanna was a good cook, and our meals together were as pleasurable as our lovemaking.

It was all very voluptuous—our being together, our enjoyment of the seasons, our enjoyment of life itself. It was all one thing, really—eating, working separately, or riding together—it was about being there with and for each other. Life was love and love was life.

For what would life be without Susanna?

I I

The Children
Michigan, 1908

She became with child that first winter. When her time came, I rode for the midwife while Maudie stayed with Susanna. The midwife was with us for two days, and brought the baby out for me to see.

"You have a fine baby boy, Mr. Burke," she said. "It was a long labor, but both Mrs. Burke and the little one are in good shape."

"We'll name him Sean, for your uncle," said Susanna as soon as I entered her room.

"Ah, Susanna, I couldn't hope for more than a healthy baby at your side, and a boy at that." I looked at her with adoration. "If you want his name to honor my uncle, then Sean it is. And I have a surprise for you."

"What is it?"

"I've hired a woman to care for the baby the first month, and a boy to help me with the harvest. We'll be able to spend plenty of time together—just you and me, Susanna—just like always."

Susanna sparkled. "Oh, Aaron, how wonderful! Now, would you please bring me the baby? I want to look at him and memorize every little wrinkle in his face."

I went to the cradle. "He's sleeping. Best not to wake him."

"You're right. There'll be plenty of time when he's awake."

Timid at first in handling my son, in no time I assumed the role of active father, although diaper changing and bathing and that sort of thing I left to the women who seemed to do them more naturally. It was the way of things then, and happy I was to turn Sean over to the nearest female.

In all honesty though, I was happiest when Sean was asleep and Susanna and I had time together, for that is when I had her all to myself, and life became quiet and sane again. I don't do all that well with a lot of people around. I like peace and quiet—at least I did then. Peace and quiet can become a nemesis if you have too much of it.

Susanna became quite tied up with Sean once the nursemaid left. It really does take all of one's time to care for a small child, and she did a wondrous job of it, always washing or cooking or cleaning or knitting new clothes for him. How she found the time to play with the little one, I'll never know; but more often than not, I would come in and find them on a blanket spread out on the floor, the baby gurgling at her while she cooed down to him. What a sight. What a woman.

The crop was good that second year, and the next year brought Eloise, named in part for my aunt. Susanna's parents came to visit. They tried to time it so they would be there for the birth, but Eloise came early, they arrived late, and by the time they arrived, she could smile for them.

A bright child, she had curly blonde hair and bright green eyes. I'm not sure where the light hair came from, as my family were the dark Irish, and Susanna's had the Irish red or brown hair with light skin you see in so many. But here came this little blondie to our house, and a beauty she was, too—so like her mother.

She laughed for the first time in her second month, a response to some tomfoolery her grandfather tried on her.

"Aaron, come see this!" called Susanna from the parlor.

Susanna, Mary and Hugh O'Connor all leaned over Eloise's cradle in the center of the room. Hugh made a ridiculous sound with his lips as if he were blowing bubbles—people do such absurd things trying to make a baby laugh—but it worked, and now I crowded around the baby with them to see her laugh from her belly each time he did it. We must have stood watching and laughing for fifteen minutes, so new was the adventure. Such a happy time.

Mary took over cooking and cleaning and helped with Sean, too. Susanna dedicated herself to the care of young Eloise, while Hugh and I worked outside.

When they first arrived, he strolled here and there on the farm. Wondering if he felt at loose ends, I called out as I walked by behind the horse. "Got some hay to bring in before it storms," I said, looking at the sky. "Care to help?"

"Sure," he said, "but I'm not quite sure what you need me doing." I showed him, and he pitched right in, happy to be of use, just like his daughter.

Funny how, up to that point in my life at least, I never had a problem finding purpose. Now I believe it was because life defined it for me. My father certainly determined my use at an early age, and in Boston, my education and paying my expenses were primary concerns. After being called back to the farm, taking care of Maudie and Susanna had been my chief task. Now I had a family to feed. Life's decisions were made with little thought on my part. Then.

Susanna's parents stayed into the fall, when they said farewell. "Now you'll be sure and visit next summer before the crops come in, won't you?" asked Mary tucking a wisp of hair back for the tenth time.

Susanna looked at me to be sure I listened. "Yes, Mama, we'll be there. All of us."

"We'll do our best," I qualified, unwilling to make promises I couldn't keep.

After they left, Susanna cried. "Oh, Aaron," she said, "they're so good to us. I miss them already."

I put my arm around her. "There now, Susanna, I'll comfort you when the going gets rough. You know that."

"Yes, I know, and I love you, it's just that..." and she began to cry again. It was a solemn day.

Aware of the load the O'Connors had taken off of Susanna and me, we were busy with the farm and the children after they left. I hired three men to help harvest the corn and wheat, and a grand harvest it was, bringing top dollar at market.

Our farm consisted of rolling countryside, more hills than valleys, and so was free of much of the frost that plagued the surrounding farms on lower land. Thus, it brought in greater crops and a good price for their prime condition. This enabled me to hire hands for planting and harvesting, bringing it in sooner for an even higher price.

I overstepped the third year, however. After a balmy March and a mild April, we decided to plant on the first of May rather than wait until the fifteenth as most farmers did. It was a mistake, and a terrible one. The frost came hard the third week of the month, withering our sprouted seedlings. Had I waited like everyone else, the seed would have been just safely planted. There was nothing to do but re-seed, which was costly.

We had to stay on top of pests that year, too, picking them off by hand at times. Hard rains came in early June. We dug trenches and ran most of the water off the fields and down the hills to the creek. Valley fields were completely washed out, having no place to send the water if no river or stream was nearby.

The only thing saving us that fall was that the valley farmers had poorer crops. Ours were needed, but prices were down by the time we got it all in, two weeks after the others. We made out all right but could not visit Susanna's family in Boston.

The children were ages one and three now. Little Sean tore into everything he could. He had more energy than any child I've seen and was difficult to satisfy and keep quiet, crying to be outside with his papa. So I tried to take him on chores, but he ran all over the place and got into things that might hurt him.

One day, for example, I was in the barn milking our cow and heard a noise behind me. The chickens began to squawk. Sean was up to something, and I said without looking, "Sean, come back where I can see you."

The sound stopped for a while, but soon started again. "Sean," I repeated louder, "over here. NOW!" When I finished milking, I turned to see that he had climbed right into the coop and broken every egg waiting to be gathered. Mischief like that I could not abide, so I left him with Susanna, followed by the sound of his howls as I went to hitch up the horses.

Sometimes I took him into town but was always sorry, for he could hardly stay in place on the wagon much less in the stores. Take my eye off him for one minute, and he was out of sight, hiding under a box or behind the meat counter looking at the guts the butcher had just removed.

When I came in after working hard in the fields all day, Sean climbed all over me. *Just leave me alone!* I wanted to say. But of course, I didn't.

As a family, we attended Mass every Sunday since my father's funeral. Susanna found a sense of community and struck up conversations with a few ladies there. But the children would not be still, forcing us to stop attending. Susanna missed the camaraderie until Maudie had an idea.

"Why not leave the children with me every other weekend so you can go? I'll attend on alternate Sundays, and we'll all get to church." The additional benefit was that Susanna and I had every other Saturday night to ourselves. I don't know how Maudie did it, but the children were happy and quiet when we picked them up after Mass, and Maudie looked happy, too.

She never mourned my father's death, of course. Perhaps she mourned the time she was married to him instead. But Maudie said it was the Lord's work she had been there for me, and I had to agree. Were it not for Maudie, I wouldn't have survived.

❖　　❖　　❖

I almost lost Susanna the following year. Expecting our third child, she was not well most of the time, having to lie down with headaches not so different from her other two pregnancies, but more severe. Often, I took over the feeding and care of the children as she lay in the next room.

One morning, before her body even had a chance to show she was with child, she rose from the bed and began to scream. I rushed in from the kitchen and looked with horror at her nightgown. Bright red covered it and the bed where she had slept. I grabbed towels and clean rags for her, but they were soaked in no time. Unable to make it stop, I rode to get the midwife, who came right away and locked herself in with Susanna, opening the door only to ask for boiling water, towels and more rags.

After several hours, the midwife emerged. "It wasn't to be, Mr. Burke," she said, taking my hand and sitting me at the table.

"But how is Susanna?"

"Your wife will pull through. I'm sorry I can't say the same for the child. I've given her a concoction to finish it off, but she must rest for a week or two. And Mr. Burke," she looked me in the eye, "be careful with her. No more babies for at least a year."

I swallowed, knowing what that meant. I paid the midwife and took her back. Susanna kept to her bed, and seven days later the bleeding finished.

Susanna was devastated, wandering at night from room to room, her pretty mouth curved downward. Once, when we were all settled down for the night, she spoke about it. "What do you think it was, Aaron?" The moon lit her face as she looked out the window. "A girl or a boy?"

I had seen a few missed births in the barnyard and didn't really wonder such things myself, so I was slow to respond. Silent, in fact.

"Do you think our little baby is still out there somewhere, wanting to come to us?" This was not a healthy direction for her mind to follow. "Or doesn't it exist anymore?"

Not good, I thought. I had better answer before she goes any further.

"Sweetheart," I began, "I don't know the answers any more than you or probably even Father James at church. I don't think anyone knows what happens when a child misses being born. But there is something I do know." She turned, her eyes fast on me, glowing in the moonlight. "You've been blessed with two beautiful children who love and adore and depend on you for everything. They miss you when you can't give them your full attention."

She turned onto her back and looked at the ceiling. "That's true. I have two wonderful, healthy children, don't I?" She sighed, rolled over and went to sleep.

Since the midwife had advised us to take a rest from childbearing, I worked more outside, spending my energy on the farm while Susanna healed on the inside. Sean and Eloise grew by leaps and bounds, both demanding their mother's full attention. Soon, as she concentrated on the children she did have, I began to see her smile more often and even laugh.

A year later, when Sean was four and Eloise almost two, Susanna was with child again. Although ill every morning and throughout most of the day, she was nonetheless happier than I had ever seen her. Convinced this was the same child that tried before, she began telling Sean and Eloise stories about the coming baby.

I came in on them as she put Sean and Eloise to bed one night. "God brought this little one back again just to be with us," she said.

"Mommy, will it be our brother or our sister?"

"Oh, only God knows that," she said. "Of course, the little one knows, too." They all laughed.

"And it won't go again, right, Mommy?" asked Eloise.

"No, it will stay with us forever and ever," assured Susanna. "God wants this little one to be with us, or He wouldn't be sending it again, right?"

"Right!" they chorused.

I wasn't sure how wise it was to give little children information we adults couldn't even be certain of. But then I thought of what they learned in church, and I wasn't sure of any of that either, so I let it go.

We moved the children to the loft, where I had built a large room for them. They were happy with their new beds and furniture, and we readied the room downstairs for the baby.

When Susanna's time came, Kathleen arrived from Boston to care for us. After an easy birth, Kathleen walked out of the birthing room smiling with little Katy in her arms. "Look, Aaron, you have a beautiful daughter!"

I rushed passed her and into the bedroom, relieved to see Susanna propped against the pillows, her beautiful hair spread out just so and a smile on her face, sound asleep.

Breathing a great sigh, I vowed this would be the last. I had seen how tired Mummy got with all of us running around all the time. Even at the age of four, I could see that. I would not saddle Susanna with a lot of children. Took care of myself after that, I did. Our lovemaking had always been tender and gentle, but I was even gentler and ever so careful after that. I would not risk losing Susanna for anything or anyone.

Kathleen stayed with us all summer, which was grand. Since our departure from Boston, Susanna and she had corresponded, but Kathleen and I had not communicated at all. I found her to be more sure of herself, a grown woman now, replete with the college diploma she had so desired.

"I want to teach," she said on her first evening with us.

"Well, congratulations, Kathleen. You'll make a great teacher," I said, thinking of Mrs. Harris.

"Do you have a position lined up?" asked Susanna.

"A few schools in Boston are looking, and I sent letters of application. If they reply, Mama and Daddy will let us know, and I'll have to return for interviews." In late August, a wire arrived calling for an interview at a school close to Aunt Louise and Uncle Sean's house. She left the next day.

Katy, suffice it to say, was the perfect child. Rosy-cheeked and dimpled, she epitomized the happy baby, crying only to signal her needs. Her eyes followed her mother around the room, and Susanna took her everywhere. Showing Katy off at church and in town, Susanna fussed over her as I had never seen her do with Sean or Eloise, who were both a little put off.

Sean, for the most part, acted up when he felt ignored. Eloise, on the other hand, stuck her thumb in her mouth and went off to sit in a corner and watch her mother play with the new baby. She was an unusual child, they both were for that matter, and I never quite understood either of them. Eloise bore an immense likeness to her mother, endearing her to me more than Sean, who more often than not reminded me of my father.

That fall, he was of an age to attend school, and I drove him to the nearest house that had children who walked to school each day. I would be there to pick him up afterward and did so until he was old enough to walk alone. It was not a bad task, but he always wanted to talk, and I just wanted peace and quiet. I'm afraid I may have been gruff with him on these rides, causing him to sulk and sour a bit.

Eloise grew and blossomed over the next few years, looking more and more like her mother except of course for the blonde hair. She followed Susanna around when Katy slept, wanting simply to be near and help with household chores. Her favorite time was when they baked cookies, she unloading them onto the pan or helping to stir the dough. As they worked together, talking and laughing, Eloise looked adoringly up at her mother.

Katy grew, too, becoming the apple of her mother's eye, however sad that was for Eloise and Sean. As much as she tried to disguise it, there was no way to mask the joy and love Susanna felt for this child she was positive had come to her twice. The bond between those two amazed me, reminding me of the bond my mother and I had. Susanna sensed in a moment when Katy awoke, waltzing into the nursery to lift her joyfully into her arms, talking and cooing to her with more affection than I have ever seen expressed by a human being in my life.

Content to see Susanna so happy, I did not involve myself with the children, although I finally did allow Sean to ride along with me during plowing or harvesting or on Saturday trips to town for supplies. Staying by my side more than he used to, he enjoyed my company more than I did his, I'm sorry to say. Children were a nuisance. I was happier letting Susanna do the upbringing while I brought in the revenue for our needs.

I 2

CRISIS
Michigan, 1916

Things changed for the worse the year Katy turned three. A dry summer followed by too much rain brought in a poorer harvest than usual. Nevertheless, once it was in and the fields plowed under for the winter, we settled in, ready again for the snow. Both of the older children, now six and eight, brought home all sorts of infirmities from school. I don't know how these things spread, but that winter we all found ourselves down with heavy chest colds. One by one we succumbed—Eloise first, then Sean, Susanna, the baby, and finally myself. It seemed to last two or three weeks in each of us then vanish as mysteriously as it had come.

Except for Katy. Perhaps because she was younger and more fragile than the rest; or maybe because she had never really been sick before and was not as resilient, Katy didn't get better in two or three weeks. In fact, she got worse and ran a temperature, scaring Susanna, who called for the doctor. Prescribing a suspension medicine for Katy's cough and salves for the pain and fever, he came out every week, then more frequently as Katy worsened.

Susanna, distraught, stayed at Katy's bedside night and day, putting soothing cloths on her forehead and giving her cool baths to bring down the fever. She brought Katy chicken broth and her favorite foods in an effort to entice her to eat. But slowly, Katy became weaker until the day came when she couldn't eat at all. By this time, the doctor was out to our house on a daily basis. No longer jovial as he had been at first, in all truth, his face had become grave, for Katy was dying.

Susanna fought it by doing everything a mother can to keep her child alive—singing songs, telling stories, holding her hand while she slept. I tried to comfort my wife as things worsened, but she became wild-eyed, rushing out of my arms and back to Katy. I let her go, of course. Couldn't force her to listen.

Finally, one cold wintry night late in February, little Katy slipped away for the second and final time, leaving Susanna behind, disheveled and unable to think straight. I let Katy go, though it was a loss for me as well as Susanna, but I had never been as attached to the little one and letting go was far easier for me.

Sean and Eloise had never seen death except for one or two barn animals. Sure, it had hit other homes in the community, but death never occurred inside our safe little household. Yet here it was. That a slight cold brought home from school could do such damage astounded us all. They were afraid, for they had not known how fragile we humans are.

Eloise blamed herself. "Daddy," she said one morning at breakfast, "I did it."

"Did what?" I asked as I poured milk for her and Sean.

"I killed Katy."

I stopped and sat down next to her. "Why ever would you say a thing like that? Eloise, you must never think you killed Katy."

She looked at me with tears in her eyes. "I brought the germ home, and we all got sick, and it killed Katy."

"You must never think that. Katy died because her body did-n't know how to fight off sickness."

"Daddy, are you sure?"

I got out of the chair, stooped down next to her and looked into her eyes. Her soul looked right back out, waiting for my answer.

I chose my words carefully, remembering what Mrs. Harris had told me after she died. "God took Katy because it was time for Katy to leave. He used her illness as an opportunity. Katy's happy now with the angels in heaven." I spoke louder so her mother would hear. "Katy isn't hurting anymore. You had nothing to do with it. Never think you did."

Eloise sat still for a moment. "Oh," she said and began to eat her cereal. That was it for her.

For Sean it was different. "So that's it then," he said one day.

"What's 'it'?" I asked.

"Life."

"What do you mean?"

"You're here, then you're gone. That easy." He sounded like a cynical old man.

"Well, perhaps for some, Sean. But it's never easy, and there's always a reason," I said, not quite as sure about the reason for such things as I sounded.

"Give me one good reason for Katy dying."

I had been wrestling with that one myself. "Sean, all I know is that we're here, and we have to take care of each other."

"What for? We're all going to die anyhow." This out of the mouth of an eight-year-old?

As he watched his mother lose her wits over this loss, he

became more standoffish and found things to do by himself—playing in his room with stick men or outside in the barn. Sean had found little comfort in the presence of humans for some time now. A reluctance to come forward and be with us had replaced his attention-motivated behavior from earlier years. I watched him develop into an aloof individual just as I had.

On the other hand, Eloise dealt with Susanna's own distancing by trying to cozy up to her mother. "There, there, Mama," she would say, forcing herself onto Susanna's lap in the rocking chair. Susanna would wrap her arms around Eloise and cry and cry. She soon saw that her mother wasn't responding to her at all, so she slid off Susanna's lap and went to the corner to suck her thumb. Other times, Eloise stood in front of Susanna and said, "It's all right, Mama, I'm here," but Susanna simply looked out the window, tears running down her cheeks.

Spring approached, and there was nothing for me to do but get out and ready the plows and hitches for planting. Plenty of fences needed mending after the vicious winter. With the children in school all day, Susanna could rest. Even so, the house was not as neat as it had been, we found ourselves hunting for clean clothes, and dinner often was not ready when we were hungry. I could not come in from the crops to do housework, and Susanna wasn't up to it. So we called on the only one we knew who could get us out of this mess.

Maudie, our Godsend, began coming every morning around nine to straighten things up and clean up the dishes. She made a fine dinner for me at noon, with plenty of leftovers for supper waiting in the oven when the children got home.

But my dear Susanna was a mess. Maudie roused her each day after the children left for school. Susanna wouldn't dress and sat in the rocker all day, eyes downcast, still as a bird the moment before it flees. We tried in so many ways to console her. Father James even came out to visit with her, but she was inattentive.

She wouldn't come out of it. One morning after trying to talk with her, I lifted her chin with my thumb and forefinger, forcing her to look into my eyes. Not a hint of recognition lay behind them. She just wasn't there. Gone. My dear Susanna no longer existed inside that lovely frame.

Distressed, I wired her parents in Boston. They, along with Aunt Louise and Uncle Sean, came out in April. Now, my aunt and uncle had never been to Michigan, and the farm was not in a condition I wanted them to see, but I needn't have been concerned.

"Aaron!" cried Aunt Louise, alighting from the passenger car. "Aaron, my dear sweet boy!"

What a relief to have them in my life again. "Aunt Louise, how good of you to come." My eyes filled as I hugged her. So much had happened since I had last seen them. My father had died. They'd never even met the two children we did have. We'd lost another. And now, Susanna herself was in dire need.

Uncle Sean stood by, allowing me my time with Aunt Louise. The O'Connor's got off the car as I released her, my eyes and nose wet and red, I'm sure. I greeted each of them solemnly and led them to Maudie's carriage.

I filled them in on the way to the farm. "The doctor says she's fine physically, but emotionally and mentally, it's another story. I think she was so attached to Katy that she just can't let her go." I explained the way Susanna had adored Katy to the detriment of her relationship with Eloise and Sean. "Eloise and Sean are suffering not just from Katy's death, but from the loss of their mother. It's like Susanna isn't in the room when she's right there in the rocking chair. Sean slips off by himself most all the time now, and Eloise sorely needs her. We all do." We rounded the drive to the farm.

Maudie had done a fine job with the house. The curtains were open when we entered, and the place looked cheery. It being Saturday, Eloise played with her dolls on the floor. Sean was somewhere else as usual, avoiding us and his mother most of all. Susanna smiled at her mother and father, her pale face lighting and my heart lifting. But then the pain returned and her tears brimmed again. I do believe Susanna's grief was so great that she had to go inside herself to keep from feeling it.

Maudie had dinner ready. We all crowded around the table, except for Susanna, who sat by the window where she had been since early morning.

"And you, Sean, what are you up to these days?" asked Uncle Sean as we ate.

Sean moved stew around on his plate with a fork. "Not much."

"Well, a big boy of eight, you must be up to something," said Aunt Louise.

"Not really."

"What do you like to do, Sean?" asked Uncle Sean. He was so interested in this place. "I'd think there'd be all kinds of things for a boy your age to do 'round here."

Sean was silent. Then, unexpectedly, "I like the animals."

This was a surprise. I knew he spent time in the barn, but I didn't know it was to be with the animals. *How like me as a boy,* I thought.

"Ah," said Uncle Sean. "Animals, is it? Have you many?"

Sean nodded. Over the years, I'd purchased two cows. We'd built a henhouse and stocked it with the finest birds for eggs and a rooster to keep them going. We had a few sheep, pigs, two horses and a mule for the work.

Not one to give up, Uncle Sean asked, "What's your favorite animal?"

"The pigs are okay."

"Do you have a favorite?"

"Yes," replied Sean, looking sideways at me now, for I had no clue to any of this. Perhaps he thought I'd disapprove, which was hardly the case.

"What's his name?"

"It's not a he. It's a she."

"What's her name, then?"

"Gertie." Gertie had been born the previous spring, about the same time Sean began spending more time in the barn. Imagine that.

"Gertie! A fine name for a pig. Did you name her?"

The others at the table smiled now.

"Eloise and I did." The children looked at each other and giggled. I was not privy to the joke.

"What's so funny?" asked Aunt Louise, almost laughing aloud at their giggles.

When was the last time I'd heard the children laugh?

"It's just that I wanted to name her Gertie, and Eloise wanted to name her Gertie, too. We both came up with the same name at the same time, that's all," explained Sean, serious again after giving Eloise a smile.

But Eloise still giggled, covering her mouth with her hand. "It was funny how it happened," she said, going into a long description of how, when the pig was born, I let each of them hold it. When I asked for a name, they surprised each other when they both said, "Gertie!" I had forgotten the whole incident and smiled now at the memory.

When was the last time *I'd* smiled?

"Well," said Uncle Sean, "I'd like to meet Gertie, if I may, after this fine meal."

"Sure," said Sean. Uncle Sean would be the closest my son would come to having a grandfather from my side of the family, and the thought choked me up.

What was the matter with me, anyway? I wasn't emotional. Susanna was the one to worry about.

"And you, Eloise, what would be your favorite thing to do around the farm?" asked Aunt Louise.

And so it went. The children warmed to their great aunt and uncle, while Susanna's parents spent time with her. They dressed her up, took her out in the buggy and forced her to sit with them on the beach. Without the strength to complain or argue, she did as they wished. But even with all that, she never came out of herself enough to talk.

Aunt Louise and Uncle Sean stayed with Maudie in town. There wasn't room at the farm for everyone, and Susanna needed her parents more than I needed my relatives. I myself was short of help and overwhelmed with the task of spring planting. Uncle Sean offered to assist, and somehow we got the crops in.

I sat down with Hugh in the kitchen a few evenings afterward. He seemed to have something to say. "Mary and I are concerned, Aaron."

I looked down at my roughened hands. Though they weren't blaming me for Susanna's condition, still I felt guilt at not being able to get her out of it.

"We think Susanna needs additional help."

I looked up. "What kind of help?"

"There's a field of medicine called psychiatry that has to do with helping the mind."

"Is a doctor like that nearby?"

"She would have to go to Chicago, I'm afraid. We could take her and stay with her."

This was not to my liking. Susanna was my wife and belonged here, with us. Yet she couldn't function, could she? It wasn't good for her here, I admitted to myself, and was unhealthy for the children to see her like this.

They sent a wire to the doctor the next day and received confirmation the day following. Aunt Louise packed Susanna's things while I stayed outside, working at avoiding the changes transpiring in my home.

Uncle Sean and I took the three of them to the station.

"We'll let you know when to pick us up," Hugh said, stepping down from the wagon.

"All right, Hugh." I ran around the wagon to lift Susanna off, so fragile was she. The porter took their luggage, then helped them up the steps and to the passenger car. Not a glance back did she give me as I stood there, wistful and alone even with my uncle at my side, and the train soon disappeared down the track.

"Ah, Susanna, where have you gone?" I asked. "Come back whole, my love. For God's sake, come back whole."

13

LEAVING
Michigan, 1917

Aunt Louise and Uncle Sean moved in with us while Susanna and her parents were gone. They had become very close to the children and were a great support for me as well. Maudie stayed at her home for the time being.

A week after the O'Connors left, we received a wire from the them.

STAYING ONE MONTH STOP THINGS GOING WELL STOP TOO EARLY TO LEAVE STOP LOVE HUGH AND MARY

A month! So long to be separated from Susanna. Yet again I reminded myself that she had not been herself for some time. I wanted the old Susanna back more than anything. It would be worth the wait.

Mary wrote twice a week detailing what the doctors (evidently more than one) were doing for Susanna. "They spend a lot of time talking," her second letter said, "just Susanna and a doctor." Amazing, since Susanna could not communicate when they left. A week later, Mary wrote, "He has her on some sort of medicine that calms her. We'll bring some back when we return."

Outdoor work was therapy for me and though new for Uncle Sean, he mended pens and fences—and anything else he saw that needed to be fixed—like a pro. This was good, as much had fallen into disrepair over the past year, and I was behind in all my work. He jumped into tasks with gusto, taking to it naturally. Uncle Sean, who dreamed of living off the land, would have made a fine farmer after all.

One evening, he and I stood outside gazing at the fields and grounds. We turned to come into the house, when he stopped.

"Aaron," he said, "looks to me like the house could use a coat of paint."

"Uncle Sean, this house has needed it ever since we moved in."

He rubbed his hands together at the prospect. "I'll bet we could have it done by Susanna's homecoming, and won't it look good!" We had it sanded and three sides done by their return.

I went to the station to get them, expecting the sick Susanna. But stepping off the car and into my arms was my old Susanna, my dear, sweet love, full of kisses and apologies. She looked into my eyes and smoothed away my tears with her glove. My dear, wonderful wife was back. I have no idea what a psychiatrist does that he could have performed such a miracle, but this was more than I had ever hoped.

Mary and Hugh glowed. The three of them filled the ride home with happy chatter about Chicago and the doctors, and how were the children, and were Uncle Sean and Aunt Louise still here?

When we reached home, the children ran out to the carriage, calling, "Mommy! Mommy!"

"Oh my darlings," she cried out, embracing them. The rest of us stood by, full of tears and smiles. A family we were once again.

While Susanna talked with the children, oohing and aahing at every story they told of their adventures with Uncle Sean and Aunt Louise, the O'Connors pulled me aside into the bedroom.

"It wasn't easy," said Mary. "Very difficult, in fact. She didn't respond well at first, you know."

"But the doctors wouldn't let her have her way," said Hugh, smiling, "and got her talking. They actually admitted her to the sanitarium for a few weeks."

I hadn't known that.

"We didn't write you that part," said Mary, "not wanting to scare you. We got to visit her every day, but the staff took care of her the rest of the time."

That evening, Uncle Sean and Aunt Louise drove back to town with Maudie. Susanna and the children went to bed early after such a big day, and the O'Connors and I sat by the fireplace.

"You know how she didn't talk here at all," said Mary.

I nodded.

"Well, by the third day of her hospital stay, she still wasn't talking. She was screaming and crying. It was really quite alarming. She looked like a wild woman, her hair all crazy."

She met Hugh's eyes. He'd aged a decade over the past month.

"But by the end of the week," said Mary, "she was coherent— crying still—but talking about her baby. By the end of the second week, we knew all about Katy."

Hugh continued, "Last week was her third, and although she still cried, she began asking about Sean and Eloise, about you and even about folks back in Boston. She asked how Kathleen was doing, and about some of her old friends." He smiled. "We knew then that she was on the road to recovery for sure."

"The doctor says she isn't out of the woods yet," warned Mary. "She needs to take her medicine and rest, he told us. Most of all, she needs to talk."

"We thought it might be good for the Father to come out on a regular basis," said Hugh.

I was stung. We had already tried the priest, but to no avail. Susanna had never needed anyone to talk with but me. I will admit she and Maudie had a good time talking over things that wouldn't have interested me. And the Father would know more about death and dying and what had happened to the baby's soul than I. Maybe it wasn't such a bad idea. "I'll have Maudie ask him to visit," I said.

The O'Connors and O'Sullivans stayed another week. Early June now, they felt the need to return home. Sean and Eloise were back to what I would call normal. It had been a good thing, this visit from our relatives, and we seemed well again.

Thank God for family.

Our life resumed a semblance of normalcy. The children finished the school year better adjusted than they had been since Katy's birth. Sean was as outgoing as he had been as a toddler, and Eloise found her mother doting on her, ironically, since Eloise had taken to doting upon her mama after Katy died. Eloise had evidently forgotten what it was to be the center of attention and didn't quite know how to behave. When Susanna did anything but focus on her, Eloise began to act exactly the way Sean had a few years prior.

"Mama, see what I'm doing," she said as Susanna washed dishes.

Susanna looked over her shoulder, smiled and said, "Uh huh."

"No, Mama," Eloise demanded. "Look!"

Susanna dried her hands on a towel, coming around the table

to look. "Oh, that's so nice, Eloise. How did you do it?"

Eloise smiled, going off into a long explanation.

Sometimes, though, it was impossible for Susanna to stop her work. "I'll be there in just a moment, Eloise."

"But Mommy, I have to show you NOW!"

"I can't, Eloise."

The girl would fall on the floor screaming, "You don't love me! You don't love me!"

"Eloise, of course I love you," Susanna would say as she continued to work, but my daughter wouldn't be pacified until her mother came over, took Eloise into her arms and gave her the attention she demanded.

Sean, happy though he seemed, continued to get into mischief. Once, I caught him riding the mule bareback in the raspberry patch, trampling the new plants and working the mule into a sweat. Another time, he hid behind the house waiting to ambush Eloise with a pail of mud. Eloise ran screaming into the house, trailing mud everywhere.

All this was very wearing on poor Susanna, who was not well yet. Beleaguered, she became drained and had to lie down several times a day to regain her strength.

In addition, I tried to resume my relationship with Susanna. "Susanna," I said one night after the children were in bed. "Come and sit beside me."

She got up and moved to my side.

"It's wonderful having you back. We missed you so."

She smiled and gazed at the fire.

"What did you do today?" I asked.

"Not much."

"Well, you made a nice supper."

"Aye."

"And I saw you washing clothes this morning."

"Aye." She really didn't hear what I said.

I became uneasy. "Susanna, look at me."

She turned, her eyes cast down.

"Look at me."

She lifted her eyes and looked into mine. It was as if a portion of her being was afraid to come out.

At first, when she came home from the hospital in Chicago, she had been all happiness and light at being back. But it became clear after a few weeks that all was not right with her. I'm sure the children picked up on it, hence their frustration in communicating with her. Something was missing, as if part of her were somewhere else, still ruminating on Katy's death, perhaps. She wasn't fully there after all.

Maudie came out to help whenever she could, but the demands on Susanna's energy took their toll, and over time, she weakened until she kept completely to bed.

And me? I was not doing well at all. To have Susanna unable to be my life partner portended a catastrophe. I needed to share my hopes and dreams and troubles with her. But she couldn't do it, and I was left alone.

Late summer, the crops Uncle Sean had helped put in matured. The children were on summer vacation, while I worked in the fields all day. Had Mrs. Harris been there, we could have had some good talks. I attempted to do so with Maudie and she with me, but it never really worked.

Evenings, I sat at Susanna's bedside. The children were settled, and I had nothing to do except mend tools. But it was all out of me, this love of taking care of the farm. I had no energy for it anymore. The love of my life could not share life with me, and I was incapable of finding purpose without her.

I wired her parents again in August.

SUSANNA WORSE STOP BETTER COME STOP AARON

They arrived ten days later.

"We'll take her back to Chicago," said Hugh as soon as they got off the train.

"Hugh, that's gracious of you, but the doctor says she's too weak for travel."

Mary cried out, "Oh, no, Aaron. Surely we can do something."

But they quieted once they saw her, for it was obvious that Susanna was in no shape to go anywhere. Her complexion yellow-gray, smudges of brown rimmed her eyes. She didn't move except to turn her head to the wall when we offered her food and drink.

She faded quickly. Finally, two weeks into November, she failed completely, leaving the children and me for the angels in heaven and her dear, sweet Katy.

❖   ❖   ❖

Kathleen and her parents came for the funeral. I had not seen Kathleen since Katy's birth, but the nature of this occasion left us little to talk about. She stayed by my side, her hand in mine, consoling me with her presence as she had after that other horrible funeral for Mrs. Harris.

We buried my beloved at the township cemetery in the woods near Glen Arbor.

Without Susanna, we did not fare well. Hugh and I brought in the crops and readied the farm for winter. The O'Sullivans stayed two weeks past the wake, trying to bring some sense back into life, but everyone was down. Maudie came out and tried to entertain the children, but they were subdued and sullen. Mary, her hair all askew, carried a handkerchief around constantly. Hugh sighed a lot, his eyes red most of the time.

Unable to cope, after everyone was asleep, I sat for hours staring into the fire. I could not care for the children, that I knew. Maudie offered to help, but even her daily visits wouldn't be enough. Sean and Eloise had always looked to Susanna for parental support, and I could not fulfill their needs. I was not a good father.

The O'Connors left before Thanksgiving. Maudie invited us to stay with her, but I didn't want to talk with anyone, so we stayed at the farm and I withdrew into myself as I had as a child. Looking back, it was the wrong thing to do, but I couldn't see another alternative at the time. The children, knowing they couldn't get any good out of me, kept company with each other instead.

The nights were the worst. I heard Eloise weep in her bed and could do nothing for her. Sean shut himself in like I did, neither of us any help to the other, much less to Eloise. I sat by the fire listening to her cry, knowing Sean was probably doing worse than I, and wondered what the hell I was doing there.

At supper one evening into the second week of our new life, I knew things had to change. Silent we were as I served up Maudie's stew. The three of us sat at the table, Susanna's place vacant as it had been since she took to her bed that past summer. We ate without speaking, all eyes on the meal before us.

This is no life for these children, I thought. I studied each of them. *My, how Eloise looked like her mother, even with her blonde hair. And don't Susanna's eyes look out at me from Sean's face?*

Seeing her so alive in the two of them was the final straw, and I broke down. It was the first I had cried since Katy became sick, and I sat right there at the table and sobbed. The children stared, their spoons poised in mid-air. I didn't stop for a long time, and neither of them said a thing. I wiped my face with a napkin afterwards and looked at them. Tears streaked their faces as well.

Sean and Eloise cleared the table, for I could barely move to the fire. Eventually they went to bed. I cried over and over at thoughts of Susanna—the way she laughed, how she looked when we met, how she loved it when we first came here, how she'd insisted on that sailboat. Unable to avoid thoughts of her, I cried anew with each one and slept not a wink.

The children managed to get themselves up in the morning, though they were late for school. Maudie came and fixed dinner, straightening up around me, clucking as she worked, for I didn't move from the fire. Never said a word to me though, she didn't. When her work was done, she left for home, shaking her head as she shut the door.

The next evening, the schoolmaster came to call.

Eloise answered the door. "Why hello, Mr. McDonald," she said in surprise. "What are you doing here?"

"I've come to see your father, Eloise. May I come in?"

I was not ready to speak to anyone.

"Daddy? Mr. McDonald's here."

Seeing me by the fire, he came in and stood by a chair I wasn't about to invite him to sit in. Who was this man to barge into my home?

"Hello Mr. Burke," he said. "I wish to convey my sympathies for your loss. May I sit down?"

I don't think I replied.

At any rate, sit he did. "Mr. Burke, there is some concern that the children are not receiving the care they need. This is the second day in a row they've been tardy for school. They've also been coming to school without being fully dressed, Mr. Burke. Are you aware of that?"

I would not respond to this intrusion. The children were lucky to even get to school, much less be perfectly dressed. He had no idea what our life was like.

After several attempts at getting a response out of me, Mr. McDonald left, saying goodbye to the children, who solemnly nodded to him then came over to sit near me.

Now, why do they sit here like that? I wondered. *Why don't they go play by themselves like they always do? And why do they have to look at me with those hangdog expressions? Why can't they leave me alone?*

I wasn't myself, you see, and it all began to boil up in me. I needed peace and quiet. I needed to be alone and didn't want to care for these children. They were so like Susanna, had her blood running through them along with mine, proof of the love we had shared. I couldn't stand to look at them, so painful a reminder were they.

"Go away," I said, but they didn't move. "Go *away*!" I shouted.

They ran upstairs, and I could hear not just Eloise now, but both children crying.

"QUIET!" I had never spoken to them that way before. "Leave me *alone*!" My voice broke.

Their cries became muffled in their pillows.

This was no good. I tromped up the stairs. "Get your coats," I said as I stuffed some clothes into a cloth sack. Their eyes big as saucers, neither said a word as I rushed them out the door. I hitched up the wagon, put them in it and headed for town.

Stopping at Maudie's, I knocked at the front door, the children still in the wagon.

"Maudie," I said when she opened it.

She looked out past me to see the children in the wagon, then back at me with alarm. "What is it Aaron?" I could tell I didn't look good from the expression on her face. I think she may have actually been afraid.

"I can't do it Maudie—" I began to break down right there on the doorstep. "You've got to take them for me."

"Here now, Aaron," she said, motioning to the children, "come in, and let's talk about it." She took my arm and pulled me in out of the cold, Sean and Eloise right behind.

"Maudie, I can't come in and sit and look at them. Please take them for me."

The children sat on the loveseat, their coats on, eyes brimming, Eloise's thumb in her mouth.

They're so little, I thought.

"Aaron, I'll do what I can, but don't you think you just need a little time?"

"I don't know, Maudie. I look at them and see her face and remember how she was and don't do anything but cry." And didn't I break down sobbing, just then.

"Grieving is hard, Aaron. You'll get through it. We all do." She paused, considering. "But it is true that the children have needs, too." She sat for a moment, then got up and took their coats. I kept mine, for I had no intention of staying. "Perhaps it would be best if you leave them here for a few days. Then we can see how you're getting along."

"Thank you, Maudie." I was out the door without a goodbye, pulling my coat up over my ears and my hat down so no one could see how broken up I was.

I couldn't face going back to the farm right away, so I unhitched the wagon behind the house and took the horse to the tavern, thinking to drown my sorrows. But speaking with towns-people I never really cared for was more than I could bear, and after an hour, I left.

I rode in the night toward the next town, where I would not be so well known. Early December it was, and the weather blus-tery. Too cold to go farther, I turned back toward home, feeling homeless nonetheless. I belonged nowhere in this world.

Reaching the farm in a far too sober state, I went straight for the liquor cabinet, emptying it over the next several days of what-ever we had put away for parties. I drained every bottle. There would be no celebrations anymore.

Maudie came out the third day, and—finding me drunk and the house a mess—turned right around and left. I'm not sure she was angry, but I do believe she remarked as she exited that she was seeing my father in me, and not his best side either.

Now I was angry. *How can she to compare me to him? Haven't I had a hard time of it? Aren't I entitled to feel the loss of my one great love?* Was this the way people were going to be? I had seen the blokes in the bar look at me, then whisper to each other. *Who do they think they are, anyway? If they're going to talk about me, they can say it to my face!*

These were the thoughts of a man sick of heart. The truth of it was that I had depended so upon Susanna for every happiness, I could not imagine being happy without her. So I closed the door on whatever else life had to offer, thinking I had no other choice.

I have no use for these people, I thought. *No use for this place.* Never had, really. We stayed here because Susanna liked it, not because of any attachment I felt for it.

I was ready to leave in two days—hired a boy to look after the animals, fixed myself a good blanket pack, got on the horse, and turned my back on the farm and everything related to the life I had lived. Trusting Maudie to wire their grandparents, I left Sean and Eloise to whatever future the relatives felt appropriate. I never wrote a note to tell of my leaving. I never said goodbye.

It was as if I had disappeared from the face of the earth.

14

TRANSIENCE
Michigan, 1916

I took the train to Saginaw and roomed at a boardinghouse for the worst of the winter. The woman who ran it fixed meals for boarders like me, men who worked the day. This would do me well, for when we sat to eat, that is all we did. Dinner conversation was about the food. "More potatoes please," or "Pass the butter." The men weren't the kind to fraternize, and that was fine with me. I just wanted to be left alone.

My room—furnished with a bed, a sturdy chair, and a night table and lamp to read by—hid at the end of the hall on the second floor. Rag rugs covered the hardwood floor. A picture of a summery country road hung above the bed.

I looked at that picture for a week, then wandered downtown. A "Help Wanted" sign in the window of a hardware store attracted my attention, and I went in. The ring of the bell on the door alerted the owner, who came forward from the rear.

He smiled and nodded to me. "Morning. Something I can help you find?" Seemed friendly.

"I saw your sign in the window and came to offer my services."

"Ah, yes, I could use a good worker." He turned to indicate the long clean organized aisles behind him. "Do you have experience?"

"I worked four years at a hardware in Boston."

"That so? Well, that would qualify as experience, I guess," he said, and we both smiled this time.

I started that day. During the week, Mr. Smith and I helped the customers. But on Saturdays, his children also worked, making the store tumultuous when it filled with shoppers.

I didn't talk to the children at all. Made me think a bit too much of the ones I had left a few hundred miles to the north. One in particular looked so like Sean, I couldn't stand to see him. Couldn't think of my own and didn't care for reminders.

I disliked serving customers and occupied myself with tasks that kept me from them. Like as not, you'd find me sweeping a corner or stocking the back shelves. Many days that hard winter no one came in at all. I liked those days the best.

Sometimes I wondered about Sean and Eloise but assumed they were well cared for. I had left most of our savings right out on the table for Maudie to see when she came out. She would make things right, would Maudie. Possibly the O'Connors would take the children. Kathleen was busy teaching school but wouldn't she want to help at night? What about Aunt Louise and Uncle Sean? Yes, plenty of people could pick up where I could no longer continue, I told myself. Never worried about them once really, though I did wonder just how they worked it all out.

By early spring, people in Saginaw felt they knew me well enough to call me by name when they came in, though I often responded in a surly manner. They nodded at me on the street and said hello at the bank when I took the day's cash. At the store, they would ask, "Could you help me, Mr. Burke? I'm looking for . . ."

The more familiar they became, the quicker I wanted to depart. By late April, I'd had it.

Taking my leave, I rode to the next big town. Flint, it was. I heard of a local farmer taking on hands for planting in early May. I got the job and lived above the stable, working all day out in the fields as I had for the past several years—away from people, out on the land. The work was hard but that was no surprise, and it felt good to be able to put something into the ground and see it come up.

The family fixed my meals, which I took in my room instead of with them. Listening to their children prattle every night would have been too much. No, it was best to keep to myself. Why, if I ate with them, they would ask where I came from and what family I might have. I didn't expect them to understand my past and didn't care to lie, so I just avoided conversation in general.

I worked for this family for three years—moving back to town for the winter, taking odd jobs only when necessary. Money from the farm job paid my winter room and board, and I pretty much holed up for the cold season.

One night deep in the winter of the third year, shouts outside of, "Fire! Fire!" awakened me. I pulled on my pants and coat and ran outdoors. Down the street, flames reached for the sky through the windows of a house as neighbors ran with buckets to put it out.

Huddled together under blankets, the poor family watched, their blackened faces streaked with tears. Their pain pierced me. I glanced at them each time I ran past for another bucket. Concern I felt, a concern that frightened me, for if I cared this much about a family I didn't know, then I must care ever so much more for my own. But I was no good for my family anymore, and I didn't do much for these poor folk either. Hard as we worked, the house burned to the ground. A fire cart arrived too late; firemen hosed the charred remains.

Mrs. Osgood, my landlady, talked to the family, her robe flapping in the wind under her overcoat. She wrapped her arms around the crying mother. "You come with me now," I heard her say. She didn't mention that the house had no vacancies. The mother looked at her husband who nodded, and they trudged down the center of the street to the boardinghouse. I trudged behind them, knowing what this meant for me.

I packed up my things and went out once again into the night. Finding the local tavern still open, I sat for a time unwilling to take a drink, remembering what it had done to me before. But after awhile, it didn't seem to matter whether I became besotted or not, and I ordered up a pitcher.

An old codger at the next table began talking. "I hear they have some wild times downtown, nights like this." We were the only two customers in the bar. Everyone else must have gone home after the fire.

I didn't reply, wasn't interested.

"What does a man do when it's nasty out?" he asked.

What kind of a question was this? Gave him the cold shoulder, I did, but he wasn't going to take that for an answer.

He brought out a deck of cards. "Ever play a hand?" An invitation, it was. Having nothing better to do, I nodded once, and he was at my table, shuffling. We played five-card stud until the place closed. I won at the beginning, but he was a sly one and had me time and again once I had plenty of drink in me. For all my ability to see through people, I neglected to look at him once. I should have. By the time we left, I had only a few dollars in my pocket and the rest of the winter ahead.

One of my dollars bought a room in the back of the saloon for the night. Waking the next morning with a terrible hangover, I was sick at my foolishness. I cleaned myself up and went out front. Getting ready to open for the day, the bartender nodded.

"Thanks for the room," I said, bag in hand. "Old Mrs. Osgood's taken in that family from the fire."

"That right?" He swept under tables, then placed chairs on the floor.

"Gave them my room, as a matter of fact."

He stopped. "Got a place to stay?"

I set my bag down. "I'm looking for one," I said, "and a job to pay for it."

He looked around the bar. Chairs sat on top of tables. The place was unswept, and it was nearly time to unlock the doors.

I followed his thinking plain as day.

"I can give you a temporary job sweeping and waiting tables, but that's about all."

"Sounds good to me." Truth was, it didn't sound good at all, but I needed a place to stay. I returned my bag to the back room.

It was the worst employment I have ever known, for I had to wait on people hand and foot. "May I help you?" I asked a pair of thugs that first day.

"Now what help could you be to us?" responded one, then laughed with his buddy.

"What would you like?" I asked a man at another table of four.

"What I'd like and what you have to offer are two different things," he said, and they roared. This was not so unlike serving Abel Chapman and that group back in the old days.

I always had the greatest disdain for types that hung out in pubs. They should be with their families or doing something to move themselves on in life, I thought, especially the ones who came in habitually. *Drunken sots.* Didn't they have something better to do?

I stopped. *Didn't I?* The pain in my heart came full force. *Hell, not anymore,* I thought. Each drunk wasting his life in the pub became a symbol of my own destiny.

After a while, I was no longer polite. Unwilling to take their barbs, I even shot back a few of my own. Now when they asked, "What help could *you* possibly be?" I retorted, "Well, looks like *you* could use *something.*"

When they said, "What I'd like and what you have to offer are two different things," I responded with, "What you'd like and what you need are even more different."

I became increasingly incensed at customers until the bartender finally pulled me aside. "Look, people complain about the way you talk to them."

"What's the matter with the way I talk? I give them what they want."

"They say you're rude, and some of the ladies are afraid of you."

"Afraid?" I laughed. "What have they got to be afraid of?"

"Listen, I want this to be a place where people can get away from their problems, a place with a nice social atmosphere. You're just not right for the job. I'm sorry, but I have to let you go."

I laughed again.

"What's so funny?" he asked.

"I've wanted to quit since the day I started. Hate serving your drunken customers. But I made myself do it because that was the job. Now you're making me do what I should have done in the first place. Quit." I took off my apron and threw it on the floor. "Who needs it?" I laughed and laughed at the joke on me.

In the end though, it wasn't so funny. In fact, it developed into another reason to move on, to stay away from people, to hate.

I had liked working warm seasons at the farm near town, but after several years, folks began to depend on me. I became a "regular," and that made me nervous. Didn't want anyone holding me down—no obligations—and I chose that moment to move out of the area entirely.

Buying a copy of the *Flint Journal,* I looked in the want ad section. A full-page ad described opportunities in booming Detroit. I headed in that direction, minding that city life wasn't for me. Outdoors was best. Nonetheless, I needed a city nearby for winter, unless I headed south where the winters were mild.

This might not be such a bad idea. Hot it was down south in the summer, but couldn't I come north to work then? End of the season here, I could go south for winter. This made a great deal of sense. I would look for new farming work here this summer, and after harvest would move south for a winter job.

Heading further south than Detroit so the trip in the fall would not be as far, I got off the train at a little farming community in central Ohio, where spring arrived earlier and summer lasted longer. I proceeded directly to the feed store across from the station. "Know anyone looking for help?" I asked the man behind the register.

A customer waiting to check out spoke up. "Why, I could use someone. Got any experience?" He hired me on the spot.

After harvest, he paid me a bonus, and I was on a train that took me all the way to Georgia. I found a room near Savannah. Hired the second day, I rode out on a wagon to a tobacco field.

Though different in many ways from farming Up North, the work was outside, and that suited me fine.

I lived in this manner for many years, going to Georgia for the winter and Ohio in the summer so I could work outdoors all year. Others did the same, some of them immigrants just off the boat as I had once been, but most from over the Mexican border.

As time went on, good workmen became harder to find, resulting in a push to hire more immigrants. Since many could not speak English, I was often put in charge of large crews.

I took care not to make friends. Human bonds brought pain. Also, I was leery of people asking questions of my past. I worked hard—that was all they needed to know.

I never spoke to women at all. Once, it had been the women in my life who had given it meaning. But I was not about to become attached to another. I simply could not chance it. The only way I survived was to put family, love and happiness out of my head and keep my nose to the grindstone.

And so, the character my father carved out years before fit me beautifully. I finally understood the man. Didn't like him. Didn't like myself for that matter. But I understood him. I was my father's son after all. Ah, me.

When I think on it now, life then and my existence after life were not so different. I had little to do with others, simply did my work. The main contrast was that, later on, I would have no work.

❖   ❖   ❖

I must have been about thirty-five years of age when it happened. Pulling a bale of hay to the loft on a farm outside Dayton, I leaned out, working the hook and pulley to bring it up and in. The bale on its way skyward swung forward, knocking me off balance. My feet went out from under me, I lost hold of the rope and went down, falling to my death.

PART II

I 5

PURGATORY
Ohio, 1922

Standing motionless by the road where I had paused on my way back to Boss Delvecchio's farm, I continued to search my soul, thinking on those who had been so good to me, wondering what I had ever done for them.

Susanna. I'd wanted so much for her to love me that I'd make the sun shine and the stars sing for her if I could, just to see the adoration and appreciation on her face.

Then it hit me. I'd wanted her to love *me*. To be happy with *me*. I'd have done anything to make her want to be with *me*.

"Just one thing," she'd said.

"And what would that one thing be?"

"We have to get a sailboat."

I remember protesting.

"Please, Aaron!"

And it was so.

Ah, the rewards. How she squealed, pulling me up, waltzing me all the way to the bedroom! Funny, how alive that scene played out in my mind as I thought about it now.

I didn't just want her happy. I wanted to be *the one* to make her happy. Why, it was selfish. I had been generous to Susanna because I wanted to be important to her.

Wasn't that natural, though?

Maybe not, I thought. Not if I resented the attention she flourished on anyone else. And didn't I resent the children because they made her happy, instead of me?

An ugly truth began to reveal itself.

Could it be that I let go of Katy more easily because she took so much of Susanna's love and attention away from me? I slumped back, appalled. The children had meant so much to her. Why couldn't I appreciate her love for them? Why couldn't I just appreciate *them*? Had I been that full of myself?

Jesus in Heaven. I was selfish in my generosity to Susanna and jealous of my own children. *Ah, no, this cannot be.* I stared at nothing for a long while as different family scenes played themselves out in my mind's eye.

I must have been generous to *someone*.

Maudie?

"I'm gonna get you out of here someday, Ronie, so you can have a good life." And hadn't she risked everything to do it? All our work for my trip when I was fifteen had been for me. And what did she get out of it? Putting up with my father all by herself while I was having the time of my life in Boston.

"Ain't no way I'd a done it differently," she'd said later. What love! What purpose!

She started me on my education when I couldn't go to school. "I'll help him," she'd told the schoolmaster, "and we'll have a grand time doing it!" Ah, she was a good one, was Maudie.

Then again, I did return to help her when my father was dying.

Hadn't wanted to though, had I? But Susanna had insisted, and, well, the decision was made for me.

Mrs. Harris. Surely I had brought some light into her world. Perhaps, but hadn't I simply responded to her love and goodness? During our visits, didn't we always talk about *my* problems? Did I ever take an interest in her life, except as it related to something for myself? Well now, there was that one time when I found out she was Jewish. Actually, that incident pointed out how little I really knew about her. No. Everything had centered around me.

Unbelievable.

And hadn't I treated the family terribly when Mrs. Harris died? Yet Aunt Louise forgave it all in a flash. "Ah, now Aaron," she'd whispered as I sobbed. "Now, now. You'll be healing, I believe." Even Kathleen had forgiven me, rude and mean as I had been.

In fact, now that I looked on it, my behavior after Mrs. Harris died was akin to my manner after Susanna went. Mean to everyone, I acted as if my grief was greater than anyone else's and no one could suffer the way I did.

Why couldn't I think of anyone else?

What had the customers told the bartender about me at the saloon? "You're rude, and some of the ladies are afraid of you." Could hear his voice plain as day.

And here I had thought myself just like the next person, moving along in what I considered to be an ordinary life. Had a family, a good farm, a lot to live for. But I really hadn't cared about any of them except for how they fit into my life. Why? Why couldn't I be interested in my own children? Why did they bother me so much?

What was the matter with me, anyway?

I became aware of my surroundings as a rider trotted by. Evening already. Then I remembered I could fly. *So what?* Where would I go? What would I do? Nothing made a difference anymore. Maybe I could throw a pencil to let my family know I was there, but what would be the purpose? I couldn't talk to them. And how would they know it was me, anyway?

Deciding to return to the cemetery, I relaxed, expecting my body to rise, but nothing happened. I kept trying, but it didn't work. Sighing, I stood up and began the tiring trek back to the place I was buried.

Days, then weeks, passed as I sat on my grave and ruminated, engrossed in thoughts about what could have been, had I cared. Worst of all was my lack of feeling for my children. They hadn't been bad. Were normal, I supposed. Sean was active as a toddler, then withdrew into himself, not unlike me. Eloise had been her mother's child. Perhaps she sensed my disdain for childish things. Certainly, I had not been the warm, loving father I could have been, but it just hadn't been in me to be like that. Still wasn't.

The people I worked for at the stable as a boy—though I did enjoy a few of the fellas there—or at the grocery as an adolescent, or even at the hardware stores, had all been nice to me, but no warmth or friendliness was in me for them. I was polite and sure to work hard to earn my pay. But the warmth had been missing.

Even way back in my childhood, I obeyed my father out of fear for my own safety and loved my mother who loved and protected me. I played with my brothers and sisters when I wanted and ran to my mother when they weren't nice to me. And didn't I love Jeremy because he loved me?

I began to think something was lacking in my character. What kept me from wanting to be around other folks? If I had been close to anyone, it was because they befriended me, not the other way around.

Even Susanna. Sure, I was in love with her, but hadn't she also been attracted to me? In fact, was I actually the one to befriend Susanna?

"She thinks you're the bee's knees, she does. Told me so herself today at Mass." Oh my, without Kathleen, would any of that have happened? If it had been up to me, would I have had the courage to court Susanna?

Ah, Susanna. I'd wanted her all to myself. Didn't want Kathleen around then or the children around later.

I was aggrieved. I had no interest in going anywhere any longer, nor did I wish to speak to anyone.

There it was. Surrounded by souls in this Second Layer—I had even seen a few in town—I kept my distance, not wanting to be bothered by anyone. I still made the choice to be alone.

Another thing. Why had I been going out to Boss Delvecchio's in the first place? To find out what he had done with *my* personal belongings. And *my* money. *My* things. The only reason I spoke to anyone at the cemetery was to find out about *my* new form of existence and what would happen to *me*—not because of any interest in them.

I was a selfish bastard. That's all there was to it.

I lay down every once in a while, for didn't all this deliberating wear me out? Then I would sit up again and consider my life, reliving the good times, reflecting on the bad ones, examining my part in it all, looking for a modicum of unselfishness in my actions and finding none.

16

LEARNING
Ohio, 1922

Blowing leaves signaled a change of season. The living wore coats, though the sun shone. For the first time in a long while, I arose, stretched and began to make the rounds of the graveyard, studying the stones. Some went back a couple hundred years. I hadn't-known this place was so old. Were settlers here then? Must have been, since I was looking at their tombstones.

I walked over to the cigar-smoking whore.

"I already told you, I'm not a whore," she blurted out before I even reached her.

"How do you know what I'm thinking?"

"Oh, come on now," she said. "You knew what people were thinking a lot of the time before you even died."

How did she know that? It was true, though. Could see right into their hearts sometimes and discern their real intentions and desires. It was one of the reasons I didn't like people.

"Well, if you'll trust that ability a little more, you can hear just about everyone's thoughts," she explained. "Not exactly word for word, 'cause it gets translated to your own thinking.

But close enough."

She was an interesting one. She knew so much.

"You'd think, me knowing so much, they'd come and get me, but it ain't happening."

"You mean, if you know enough, they'll come and get you?"

"Not exactly," she said, becoming exasperated again. "You gotta *learn* about yourself. That's what they say, anyway. I've talked to a lot of folks here. They've seen others go over after they learned about what they did wrong and all."

Well. I knew why they weren't coming to get *her*.

"What's so wrong with me, if you know so much? What do you know that you ain't telling?"

I couldn't think a thought without her hearing it. Didn't like that.

"I'll tell you how to keep your thoughts from other people, but first tell me why you think they ain't coming for me. And just *think* the answer to me. You don't have to say it."

Well, I thought, *it's your temper.*

"Oh," she said. "Yeah. I know about that. Got a bad one. It's gotten me into trouble more than once," she admitted.

Clearly, she had heard my thought. Astounding.

You're so impatient when I don't understand what you say, I added.

"All right! All right! I know I'm impatient, but I can't stand it when I say something loud and clear, and someone is too stupid to hear it."

"I'm not stupid."

"Sorry, but you sure seemed like it when I first spoke to you."

"But it was hard to understand what you were saying to me. Coming straight from the living, this is a lot to absorb."

She sighed. "Yeah, I guess it is. Been here so long, I figure what's obvious to me is obvious to everyone. I forget how long it took me to learn." She moved her toe in the dirt, studying it. "I do that a lot." She thought for a moment. "There's a word for that, when you can see things from somebody else's shoes or whatever. Can't think of it."

"Empathy." My education with Mrs. Harris was paying off, even here.

"Yeah. Empathy. It's what I haven't got." She looked up, smiling again. "Got everything else, though!"

"Well, if you know it, shouldn't they be coming to get you?"

She sighed, calming herself. "It ain't that simple. You gotta learn about yourself, then you have to fix it."

"You have to *change* yourself?"

"You got it!"

"Oh." The weight of it hit me. I would stay like this until I changed my character.

"They say that's what life is for, so you can grow and all that good stuff. If we don't do it during life, we get to do it afterward."

"Oh." *My.*

She saw my shock. "Oh, come on, now," she consoled. "You don't have to change everything. Like they say, nobody's perfect. And somebody said you still get to change stuff in Heaven, too, or wherever the hell it is we go. But those of us with more to work on stay behind. Then there's the ones who don't *want* to die—they don't go over either," she added.

"You mean, if someone wants to live, and they die, they become . . . like us?" I didn't want to say "ghosts." Wasn't ready to admit I was one.

"Not exactly. Nobody wants to give up life." She stopped and corrected herself. "Well, there's the suicides. But others refuse to go on, too. They just want to be left alone. Like you. So they're here for a while till they decide they're ready to be with folks again."

"But I'm not alone. I'm with you." I gestured around to the others. "And them."

"And there's a bunch more like us all over the world," she said. "But we all give one another space. Once you're here for awhile, you'll see there's something wrong with each and every one of us. Worse than them." She indicated the town, where the living were. "And who wants to get involved with people that ain't quite right?" She sighed. "So we stay away from each other." Her smile acknowledged that we weren't doing what she'd just said. "Pretty much."

"Do you want me to go away?" I asked, stepping back.

"Not necessarily," she said. Then, "Oh, you want to protect your thoughts from the rest of us?"

I nodded.

"Just put a big bubble around you."

I looked at her, confused.

"Like when you fly, remember how you sent yourself forward?"

I nodded, noting that she didn't lose her patience with me this time even though I wasn't getting it. She sensed the thought and smiled.

"Just send that out, but all around yourself at the same time. It'll shield you from everyone hearing your thoughts."

I tried it.

"All around you. And you'll find you have more energy, 'cause you're not picking up nothing from any of them, either."

She gazed toward town, and I could see it was time to go. I got up and began to leave.

"Hold it there a second so it'll seal."

I stood and tried again. It was like blowing a balloon around me with my energy and holding it there.

Thanks, I thought, but she didn't hear me. Had her bubble up already. Or maybe mine was working. Too late, I realized I still didn't know her name.

Typical, for a body who cares only about himself.

Funny that a whore would have so much to tell someone like me. Made you wonder how a smart girl like that could end up in such a disreputable profession. You'd think she would know better than to even get started that way, but maybe it hadn't been her fault. Maybe it had been forced on her. One never knew.

"Wasn't like that at all." She stood beside me.

"Why do you keep doing that?" I asked, perturbed by her lack of respect for a person's privacy.

"Hey," she said, "if you don't have your bubble up after you know about it, I figure you're fair game." Then she looked off into the distance. "It really was my fault, you know."

I had no idea what she referred to.

"I was young, angry." We both smiled. "All right, I've always been angry. Was angry when I was a little kid, too." She sat down next to me. Surprisingly, I didn't mind the interruption.

"My dad, he was kind of like yours," she said.

I looked at her in surprise.

"Hey, you were doing all that thinking before you knew about the bubble, remember?"

Oh, I thought. *Hmmm.*

"Mine was a mean one. Expected me to behave a certain way for other folks that just wasn't me. I wasn't gonna do it. Was downright defiant." She was silent a while. "By the time I was sixteen, I'd had it. Wouldn't go to church with him and act all prissy like everyone else. Got tired of always putting on a show of being The Perfect Child when I got a kick out of being so nasty the rest of the time.

"So I slipped outta my window one night and went to the local whorehouse. Thought I'd show him. Really, I was scared to death. But the girls were so nice. They laughed when I complained about how prim and proper he wanted me to be and took me right in. Didn't make me work or nothing till I was ready."

She looked down at her toe, pushing at the dirt. "Don't make moral judgments about us girls who go into The Profession." She looked over at me. "I never made judgments about you."

"And why would you be making judgments about me?"

"Well, that'd be easy. I know you abandoned..."

I was on my feet. "ENOUGH!"

"Well, ya did!"

"And you're not making moral judgments? Ha!" I snorted and walked off.

She was beside me. "I know what you did," she said, "and I know why you did it."

I looked at her but kept walking.

She stayed right alongside. "I'm not a snoop. You were loud and clear with your thoughts."

"So you know what I did and why I did it. What business is it of yours?"

"I'm just telling you. Even though I know, I'm not making

judgments." She turned surly. "I don't care, really. Got enough of my own troubles to think about without worrying about yours!" and she vanished. She wasn't at her grave or anywhere in the cemetery.

"Hey!" I shouted. "What's your name?"

No answer.

Putting up my bubble, I went back to my grave. Who was she to tell me what I did and didn't do and put names on it? Wasn't that a kind of judgment, when you put words like "abandoned" on what a person did? Weren't you putting it in a category with other bad things?

Chafing at the effrontery of it, I sank into myself again, thinking about what I had done. And what I hadn't done. And what I could have done. And what I should have done. I thought and thought until it all became a muddle, and I—miserable. Ah, for the likes of me, I didn't know anymore what was right or wrong, so I laid back down and closed my eyes.

❖ ❖ ❖

Time flew in the Second Layer. Winter it was, and though I didn't feel the cold, the sight of it made me wish for the sunlight of the South. To stay in this ghastly place for the winter was not a happy thought. I would have to go into complete hibernation like some of the fools around me, just to get through it.

She popped up on one side of me. "There you go again," she commented, "making moral judgments about all us 'fools' who stay here." She disappeared.

"Truth is"—she was on my other side now—" you don't know why we stay, do you?" And she disappeared again.

I lost patience with her shenanigans. *Time to go somewhere else,*

I thought as I rose and stretched, trying to recall the point of going South. I considered a trip to see my children in Michigan instead. It was winter there, too, but I could be indoors, couldn't I? Just didn't want to feel the wind and ice and snow, although the temperature and dampness didn't bother me. Interesting how the blowing textures of rain, ice, and sleet did, though.

I decided to see if I could fly. Hadn't tried since that day by the road months ago. Closing my eyes, I relaxed and willed myself into the air. Up I went. Hovering, I looked around.

She floated beside me. "Where're we going?"

"I'm the one who's going. You can do what you want."

"You missed it, by the way," she said, fiddling with her nails, then looking off into the distance as if what she said weren't important.

She had me. "Missed what?"

"Well, look." She pointed at the grave with the tired old woman always lying on it. Except the old woman wasn't there.

"Where is she?"

"They came and got her," she said with satisfaction. "Two hundred years, and they finally came and got her." She nodded, bright and dreamy-eyed once again. "Was a sight to see, too. Sky all lit up, hundreds of them waiting on the Other Side. She just got up and walked over to them like she wasn't tired at all." She sighed and looked at me. "Too bad you missed it." And she was gone.

Enough of her. Enough of this place. Propelling myself over the gates, I stopped and turned, looking back one final time at the only spot on earth I could say truly belonged to me. I shook my head. Who needed it?

"Hey." She was beside me again. "Name's Marnie." And finally, she vanished for good.

❖   ❖   ❖

I couldn't fly as well as Marnie. Seemed she could move from one spot to another in an instant. Not me. Fighting the wind fatigued me, and I struggled when I got tired, so I stopped often to rest.

It fascinated me though, as I flew over cemeteries like my own and saw ghosts resting by graves. Other ghosts—all kinds of them—moved among the living. All ages, too. Children, adults, old folks. Animals in our layer mixed in with crowds of living people or sat alone, watching humans go by. One wonders why an animal would be a ghost.

I didn't acknowledge any of them, of course, and they didn't acknowledge me. Marnie was right about that. We stayed away from each other.

As I made my way to northern Michigan, the weather became more severe, and I napped more often. After what must have been weeks—time passed so quickly when I rested, it was hard to tell—I finally reached Leelanau County. The sun was out and not a cloud in the sky. No wind, either, which made it a particularly fine day for flying.

I didn't recognize the farm from the air at first but finally located it and landed in the front yard. Deserted it was, its windows boarded up and the barn empty, not a sign of life around.

Of course! They must be in town for the winter. I headed for Maudie's. Her house glowed, all lit up like Christmas without a tree. Quite a few people were gathered inside, and I entered through a window. I thought at first that it must be a party, then noticed the silence. Everyone was somber, sober, sullen.

"Won't be long," said old Mr. Applebee.

"Hush," said his wife.

I walked to the bedroom. Several people sat on small chairs placed around the bed. I floated closer. There she was, pillows fluffed behind her head, her face a pasty white covered with a sheen of sweat. Maudie was dying.

Sean and Eloise were not in the room. I wanted to look for them and examined Maudie to be sure she would remain alive while I searched the house. But her chest rattled, and she worsened before my eyes. After a while it rose one final time, then fell, her life leaving on her breath.

Then the most extraordinary thing occurred. Still lying down, she rose out of her physical body, sat up and looked about. Nearly to the ceiling now, she looked down at her body in the bed and all the mourners at her bedside. Before she had a chance to become alarmed, the ceiling opened to a great light, the walls evaporating in its brilliance. A luminous form deep inside the light came forward, reached a hand to her, and she stood, walked a few steps and took it. Together, they disappeared into the dense brightness, which gradually dissipated until nothing was left but ceiling and walls once again.

I was stunned. People in the room cried as they viewed her remains. Why? Hadn't they seen it? But then, I was crying, too. I had seen something truly remarkable. This is what Marnie had talked about. Maudie had crossed over, and I, a witness.

I sat in an empty chair and wept. *Oh, God,* I prayed, *let them come for me, too.* I cried and cried, thinking how wondrous to have witnessed this event, how terrible to be left behind.

When I came to myself, the room was clean, the shades up and curtains open, body and visitors gone. Ah, I was tired—tired of this wretched existence. I had glimpsed magnificence. They had come to get Maudie—but not me. Desolate, I stayed in that room all winter.

17

REVISITING
Michigan, 1923

I jerked awake. The slant of the sun told me it was spring. Time to get the plow ready, mend the fences, buy seed. But not for me. Never again for me.

I missed sowing the seed, watching it sprout and grow, helping the plants survive, the accomplishment of the harvest. I missed the happiness it had brought the family and me. I missed my family. I missed the warm little home Susanna had made for us.

No, I told myself. *Enough wallowing in misery. Time to go out.*

I flew the few miles to our old home, now completely overgrown. The fields had gone to seed, and the natural growth my father and I had worked so hard to clear was all back. This place hadn't been farmed in years, probably not since I left. Its fertile soil had produced a good yield every year except that last one with the drought and the blight. And now look at it. What a waste.

That last year—what a horrible time it had been. And not just for me. Poor Susanna. And Maudie had worked so hard. And the children—what must it have been like for them?

Just where were the children? If they weren't here at the

farm...they must be...

Oh. My. Boston.

It had been hard enough coming from Ohio to northern Michigan. Flying to Boston would take months. *Months.* And so exhausting.

The shock of seeing the farm in this condition debilitated me for sure. I decided to rest first, but by the following week was ready to move. Taking my time, I flew over Michigan's swamps and fields; over farmers planting crops and children playing in yards; over burgeoning cities and heavily trafficked intersections; around high buildings; over lakes, rivers and streams. I enjoyed the journey, relaxing when I needed to. There was no rush, no deadline, no desperation. I would be in this state of being for a time, it seemed. I might as well enjoy what aspects of it I could.

After a while, however, the trip began to fatigue me. Just when it began to seem interminable, the landscape changed to mountains and beautiful waterfalls. I stopped for several days and lay alongside a river, listening to it bubble before it dropped hundreds of feet to the pool below. It was remarkable how long I could stay in a place and do little when I'd been so accustomed to working hard in life.

Moving on, I finally came to the rocky hills surrounding Boston itself. How the town had grown since I had last seen it! I found Canterbury Street and my aunt and uncle's house, then flew in. Walking around the premises, I even visited the garret I had once called my own. It held two beds but no people.

Where was everyone?

Taking a look down at the O'Connors, they were gone, too. I still had my sense of smell and perceived something cooking. Checking in the kitchen, I found a chicken roasting in the oven.

Someone should be watching over it, I thought.

Then it hit me. *It must be Sunday!* They were in church! Rapturous, I lifted my way to the cathedral, and hearing organ music, entered.

People from years ago sat facing the priest. Aunt Louise, in a very large hat, and Uncle Sean in the O'Sullivan pew—older, but still in good health. Dear Kathleen, intent upon the words of the priest. Next to her sat a gentleman I had never seen. He looked a good sort, dressed in a brown suit, a matching hat setting on his lap. Next to him were two adolescents—a blond girl and...

Eloise and Sean. How grown up they'd become! I tried to count back in my mind to the day I left but had lost track of the years. Surely, these were my children. Eloise, the picture of Susanna. Beautiful. My heart ached watching her tender face as she listened with rapt attention to the priest. Sean, next to her, looked to be fourteen or so and less than enthralled with the sermon. I chuckled. His hair nearly disciplined into place, he wore a nice suit. Again, his dark looks reminded me of my father, chilling my insides. I hoped he didn't carry the disposition with it.

In my travels, I had mulled things over, coming to the understanding that I myself had indeed become just like my hated father. Perhaps I hadn't bossed the children around as badly—at least not until that last horrible night—but I had been irritable, demanding things go my way. I was happy only when Susanna, bless her heart, did my bidding. She was good at that and thus kept peace in the house.

Ah, Sean, I thought, *take a little goodness from your uncle next to you and don't be like me.*

I looked across the aisle to see Hugh and Mary O'Connor holding hands. Would that be Susanna's brother next to them, with perhaps a wife and children? *Ah, no.* I could not bear to look further to see the rest of them.

Susanna, Susanna. Where are you, my love? Looking at these faces, I miss you even more.

Everyone pulled out hymnals and thumbed pages. When they stood to sing, I lifted to watch from above. A whole new perspective of hats and heads, it was. Sean didn't attempt a note; Uncle Sean mumbled into the hymnal; and Hugh gazed off into space. But the women sang out, I will say that.

Then it was over. People poured into the aisle, waiting for those in back to exit. I didn't blame them. The place was cloying. Father O'Brien greeted each parishioner at the door, making it a lengthy wait for the rest. Looking back at the family, I caught a glimpse as Sean left by a side door and followed to see what he was up to.

Four or five boys had grouped together behind the church. Sean arrived, and they passed him a smoke. Amazing. In church one moment, breaking rules the next. What had become of this boy? Their conversation centered around this or that girl, what she had said, what she would do. Boy talk. Big talk. I smiled to myself, until the subject of Eloise came up.

"Your sister thinks she's a queen," said a smart aleck.

"And how!" agreed Sean. "She gets everything she wants from Kathleen. Cozies up to her, acts real nice and gets her way every time."

"Why don't you try that?" asked another boy. "Might work."

They laughed.

"I don't have the patience for girl stuff. You gotta sit around and listen to everything they say and practically act like it's God's word," he answered. "I can't stand to be around them." He inhaled the smoke then blew it out in rings. Pretty good ones, too.

"Better get used to it," said the second boy. "Someday, one'll snag you. Once you're married, you'll have to cozy up for all your needs."

"Yeah," agreed the others, sniggering.

A pair of adults rounded the corner. The boys threw their cigarettes into the bushes and stepped apart, allowing the smoke to disperse.

"Well, how are you boys today?" asked the gentleman.

"Fine," the boys mumbled, clearly unwilling to converse.

"Alexander, it's time to go home," said the lady, and one of the boys trudged off behind her, head down, looking back once at his buddies, waving desultorily.

"That kid would have it made if he'd just get out and have some fun once in a while," said my son. "One of our midnight adventures, and he'd be a new man."

Midnight adventures?

"Yeah," laughed another. "Hey, what's up for tonight?"

"Danny and Jerry and I thought we'd go downtown and see if we can pick anything good up," said Sean.

My son, at age fourteen, picking women up off the street? Why, he could get in trouble or—or contract a disease! What kind of life was he setting up for himself, doing things like this?

I turned away to find Eloise. Lifting up and moving to the front of the cathedral, I was taken aback at the sea of hats bobbing in conversation below. In amongst them, I found a hatless Eloise talking with the family. They all laughed.

"We expect great things from you some day, Eloise. Your pictures are lovely."

"Thank you, Uncle Sean," she said, "but they really are just beginner's work."

"Keep it up, my dear, and you will succeed."

"Anyone seen Sean?" asked Kathleen. They looked about.

"I'll check out back," said Kathleen's man friend. He wore a wedding band. *Well, now.* So Kathleen was married.

"He's looking better, Kathleen," said Susanna's mother, once he was out of earshot.

"He's making headway," agreed Kathleen. "The doctor says it could go either way, so we'll just have to wait and see. And pray."

What was the matter with her husband?

"Never hurts to put in a word Upstairs," agreed Uncle Sean.

Eloise looked troubled, her eyes downcast. "He won't die, will he Kathleen?"

"Oh, now, now." Aunt Louise put her arm around Eloise's shoulders. "We mustn't talk like that."

Kathleen drew in a long breath. "I don't think so, Eloise."

"Of course he won't die," said my mother-in-law. "He's quite strong. You can see that."

Sean and Kathleen's husband came around the corner, talking and laughing together. Their obvious pleasure in one another made me uncomfortable. How had this man befriended my son?

"Found him up to no good."

"Not true, Josh!" countered Sean, laughing. "Just talking, is all."

"Ah, but the subject matter," replied Josh. "That is a different thing." He winked at Kathleen, who perked up.

"All right, Josh. No need to go prying into Sean's conversations," she said. I wondered if she truly was overly protective of Sean, as well as Eloise. "Let's go home and have dinner."

Separating into two groups, the O'Connors walked home with my aunt and uncle, while Kathleen and Josh left with Eloise and Sean in a horseless carriage. As they passed her parents, Kathleen leaned out and said, "We'll be over around two." Uncle Sean and Aunt Louise acknowledged with a wave, and off they went.

I floated behind the carriage as we traveled across town to a newly developed area. We stopped in front of a large, white two-story home with a pillared front portico. Josh took the carriage around back while the others went in. The children ran upstairs, each to a separate room. Kathleen removed her bonnet and went to the kitchen.

So. They were with Kathleen after all. It made sense. Didn't she always want to fix people's lives? Why wouldn't she be the one to take in the children? I had discovered what I needed to know. My children were well cared for by my family, though not exactly as I had expected. My relatives were fine.

But I was not ready to leave. I wanted to know what Sean was up to. What kind of painting did Eloise do? And what was the matter with Kathleen's husband? Why not stay and find out? What else did I have to do?

Curious as I was about my children and life in Boston, I had no choice but to rest. Finding a place under an old willow in Kathleen's backyard, I lay my head down and closed my eyes.

When I opened them, evening it was, and rain poured down. How much time had passed? I meandered to the parlor window to have a look-see. A doctor, the telltale valise at his feet, engaged Kathleen in conversation. Entering through a window, I thought this must be about Josh.

"You must be cautious, my dear," the doctor said. "It's best to keep him out of any draughts and bad weather whatsoever."

She listened, somber but not sad.

They stood up, and he reached for his bag. "Things look better," he concluded. "We want to keep them that way."

"I will, Doctor."

"And don't let the children wear him out. I know he's fond of them, but he is very easily exhausted."

"I'll make sure their visits are short."

"We're out of the woods, but it's a long journey back to complete health. I'll come by the same time next week," and he left.

Kathleen turned and ran up the stairs. I followed as she scurried down the hallway and into the back room where Josh lay in bed, looking much worse than he had at church.

How much time had elapsed?

"Oh, Josh!" she exclaimed, sitting next to him. "He says you're out of the woods! Isn't that wonderful?" She leaned over and kissed his forehead.

Josh smiled. "Told me the same thing."

She clapped her hands together. "Won't be long, and you'll be up and around, working and doing all the things you like. Won't that be grand?" asked Kathleen, The Fixer, who had to have everything working the way it should.

"Well, right now, I'm actually kind of tired," he responded, sliding under the covers.

She jumped up. "Oh! Well yes, you must be, after the doctor's visit and all." She smoothed the blankets. "You have a nice nap, and I'll come up later to see how you're doing." She picked up a cup from the bedside table, turned out a lamp and left.

I went to search for the children in the other bedrooms. Clothes were strewn about in one. Unfinished schoolwork sat at a lighted desk in the other. But Sean and Eloise were not there. After checking the attic, I went downstairs, where Kathleen was busy sewing in the parlor.

A moment later, in walked the miscreants with Uncle Sean. They removed their rain gear and hung it on a hat rack by the door, then came straight into the parlor.

Kathleen put down her work. "Oh, there you are, you three!"

"What did he say, Kathleen?" asked Eloise, anxiety on her face.

"Hi Daddy," said Kathleen, as her father kissed her cheek. They all sat down. "Well, it's good news!" She laughed as their faces lit up. "He's out of the woods but still has to be careful to stay out of bad weather and draughts. And I'm not to let you two tire him out!"

"Oh darling, I'm so happy for you," said Uncle Sean.

"Hurray!" shouted Eloise.

"Did he say how long it'll be before we can go out and fool around together?" asked Sean.

"If we take good care of him, he'll be out doing 'stuff' with you in no time."

"This is indeed good news, Kathleen," said Uncle Sean.

"It is, Daddy, isn't it?"

Eloise rose. "Well, I've got to get some homework done. Goodnight, Uncle Sean. Thank you for the sundae. Goodnight, Kathleen," she said, kissing them, then climbing the stairs.

Kathleen resumed sewing. "Sean, how about your homework?"

"Aw, I finished it at school," said Sean. "But I've got a book to read, so I'll do that," and he was up the stairs before they could say goodnight.

Kathleen and her father sat in silence for a moment. Uncle Sean took out a pipe, asking, "Mind?" Kathleen shook her head. He lit it and sat back, squinting as he peered into space. "I'm happy for you, Kathleen, that he's pulling through like he is. Wasn't clear for a while that he would."

"It didn't look good, did it, Daddy?"

"Well, the important thing now is that he gets enough rest and care." He smiled. "You'll see to that, I know."

Uncle Sean became more serious. "There's another matter that concerns me, though." He puffed on his pipe. "Been hearing stories from a few folks about Sean and his shenanigans."

She put down her work. "What kind of stories?"

"Stories you don't want to hear but have to know for the good of the boy." He shifted in his chair, leaning forward to speak more quietly. "Seems he's out all hours of the night, tearing around town. My friend, Johnnie McConnaghie at the station, tells me he sees him outside some of the worst pubs. Broke up a fight between him and some others one night and sent him home. Came 'round to tell me of it the next day, and I've been waiting for a good time to share it with you. Now that Josh is better, maybe you can take a good look at what Sean is up to."

"Well Daddy, I didn't want to worry you, but a policeman did bring him home one night—must have been a year ago—and Sean and I had it out then. I thought he'd learned his lesson."

"Point is, we're going to have to keep him on a tight leash."

Kathleen sat still, thinking. "He always goes to his room at night and never comes out again," she said as she rose. "The front door is locked and bolted, so he can't get back in that way." She rushed to the stairs.

"Where are you going?"

"To see if he's there." Quietly, she ran up the steps. After two quick knocks, she entered his room, walked to the slightly open window and looked out at the empty street.

Returning to the parlor, she said, "It's the tree outside his window he climbs, I'm thinking."

Her father stood. "Well, I have a few friends at the station. I think I'll see if we can't find that boy."

"Oh, Daddy, I'm sorry."

"Kathleen, this isn't your fault. You're doing the best you can. Remember. This boy came to us with problems. You didn't create them," he said. "Don't take any of this on yourself. The one to take it on isn't here, or he'd be the one going to the station."

What?!

Kathleen defended me. "Aaron had too much to handle, Daddy, you know that."

"Ah, but Aaron had responsibilities he didn't live up to," said Uncle Sean, his voice rising. "You don't go off and leave two children just like that! Didn't even say goodbye." He walked to the door. "A person just doesn't do that. And look at them now." He grew more vehement. "Eloise worries every time someone gets sick for fear she'll be abandoned again, and Sean out God knows where in the middle of the night."

He was angry now. "The man should be shot for abandonment," he raised his finger, "*if* they ever find him." He shook his head. "The way we took him in and all." He walked out the door.

"I'll let you know what I find," he called from the sidewalk, muttering as he strode away.

Kathleen watched at the door until he disappeared. Shivering, she hurried back in, checked Sean's room once more, then knocked on Eloise's door.

"Come in." Eloise lay sprawled on the floor intent on cutting a scrap of paper for a school project.

Kathleen sat down on the bed. "That's nice, Eloise. What's it for?"

"It's about the different properties of matter. You know— solid, liquid and gas." She pasted the newly cut form onto a large cardboard square, then held the entire work up for both to see. "There, I'm finished." She stood and stepped back, studying it.

"You've done a fine job," approved Kathleen. Softening her tone, she said, "Eloise, I have something to ask you."

My daughter's eyes shone as she turned to look at Kathleen with love. "Whatever it is, I'll do it." Thank goodness she had found someone she loved to share this part of her life. I was so relieved that I sat down next to Kathleen. They didn't notice the dent I made in the bed covers. Neither did I.

"Do you know where your brother is?"

Eloise looked with surprise at Kathleen. "Whatever are you talking about, Kathleen? He's in his room, working."

"Well, he's not there."

"What?" Eloise jumped up, ran out of her room and into Sean's. "You're right!" she cried as she returned. "You didn't see him leave?"

Kathleen shook her head.

"Then where is he?"

"That's what I'm trying to find out."

Eloise sat on the other bed. "He told me a long time ago he'd wring my neck if I ever set foot in his room, so I don't."

"He said that?"

"Oh, that's nothing, Kathleen. He hates me. Hates just about everybody, except his buddies and Josh."

"What do you mean, he hates you?"

"He does. Tells me so all the time. Says I better stay out of his way—that what he does and where he goes is none of my business. He's always been like that."

"Always?"

"Ever since we were little. He was always going off some-where, not wanting anyone to bother him." She paused, deep in thought. "He used to like Uncle Sean but thinks he's an old stick-in-the-mud now." She looked at Kathleen, worried that she had said too much. "I'm sorry, Kathleen. You wanted to know, right?"

Kathleen straightened, her mouth set. "Yes, I wanted to know. What I don't know is how I missed it."

"Missed what?"

"The way Sean feels. I thought his attitude was normal for a boy his age. I didn't realize he hated us all so much. Or that he sneaks out. We did everything we could . . ." Her voice trailed off.

"Oh, Kathleen," said Eloise, moving to sit next to her—right where I sat! I got up quickly to make room. Didn't like it when people took my space. Just wasn't comfortable.

"That's just the way Sean is. There's nothing anyone can do about it." Eloise was matter-of-fact. "Well, one person could do something about it, but he's not here."

Oh, no. She wouldn't blame this on me, too, would she? Young Sean had problems long before I left. It was one of the reasons he'd been so difficult to care for even then!

"Aye," said Kathleen, falling back into the Irish lilt, "if he were to appear on the doorstep again, it might make all the difference in the world for Sean." Her eyes were far off.

"For me, too," Eloise said, then grew defiant. "But I'm not sure I'd be happy to see him after the way he left us with Maudie, and nobody knowing what to do. Made Gram and Gramps come and get us." Her face softened. "Good thing *you* wanted us."

"Of course we wanted you," Kathleen said, putting her arm around Eloise, pulling her close. "I've always loved you, remember?"

Eloise nodded. "Unlike some people."

So they are *blaming me,* I thought. I whisked out of the room and out of the house.

"What was that?" asked Kathleen as I passed.

"What was what?"

"I don't know," said Kathleen, shrugging, and they both giggled.

Ah, what's the point? I asked myself as I lay down out back under the old willow. What did I hope to accomplish, peering into these lives long after I'd left them? Things were the way they were going to be, and I could do nothing to change any of it. That was a fact.

I was drained. That was a fact, too. The exertion of slowing down to observe them did me in. And what satisfaction I'd received from seeing my almost-grown children was quickly changing to disappointment. Sean was certainly not the epitome of the perfect child. And did I have to listen to my daughter complain about my role in all of this? I didn't have to put up with this!

At least Kathleen defended me. I could get a modicum of satisfaction out of that. And that they actually needed me long after I was gone. If they had been completely fine without me, I might not be entirely happy either. So, then. There could be no comfort from seeing my children at all. If they were doing fine, I would translate it into their not needing me. If they were doing poorly, believing it was because I was not with them, then I'd be angry and blame them for not understanding.

Well, the fact was that they were doing poorly precisely *because* I had left them. That they were angry with me did not change that. True, Sean had not done well even when I lived with the family, but would he have done better if I had taken more of an interest in him? Surely, that would have helped.

I remembered the way he opened up to Uncle Sean about

Gertie when Susanna was ill, but Uncle Sean seemed more judgmental now. Perhaps my son saw that his uncle was not predisposed to accept misbehavior. Bigger boys misbehave in bigger ways and are not so cute after awhile.

I closed my eyes. Life was wearisome. I was glad mine was over.

18

FORGIVENESS
Boston, 1924

I can't say we sleep in this Second Layer. It's more like the lights go out and no one is home. And yet, if someone were to cry out, we would surely come to. Upon opening our eyes, months or even years may have passed.

Which was exactly the case when I came to myself again. Awakened by a scream, I jumped up, sure that someone had seen me. Then Kathleen, Josh, Eloise and another young man I did not know ran out to the yard—not to my tree, but to the tree just outside Sean's window. Sean lay on the ground below, his young body awry, just as mine had been when I died.

Oh, Sean, I thought. *Not already. You're far too young to go.*

"They go at any age," said a voice at my side.

Marnie? I looked about but didn't see her.

I went to examine the body, which indeed appeared to be dead. Had his spirit already crossed? Had I missed that?

"He's over there," said the voice. Somehow, I knew "over there" was away from the house to the far end of the yard where a figure walked among last summer's dead flowers.

Ah, Sean, I thought.

He looked up. "I don't get it."

I greeted him as I approached. "Sean."

He stopped and scrutinized me. "Dad?" He began to tremble. "Dad?" The shaking increased, as his expression changed to one of anger. "So," he said, "you finally came back. A little late, aren't you?" The words sounded strangely familiar.

"Sean, I'm . . ." Now I was the one confused. "I'm so sorry."

He motioned a shaky arm to the body, now surrounded by a crowd. "Took them long enough to find me. Happened early last evening. It's almost dawn."

He began to pace again. Stopping, he looked at me, then asked, "You were dead, weren't you?"

I nodded.

The condemnation in his eyes vanished. "For a long time? Is that why we never knew where you were, because you were dead all this time?"

"Not . . . the whole time," I admitted.

"So. You *did* abandon us." He smiled cynically as he resumed pacing the garden's perimeter. "We all knew it."

He stopped again. "What happens now? Do we just hang a-round like this?" He indicated his body over there, then himself in the Second Layer.

"For awhile. Someone will come and get you, sooner or later."

"Sooner or later? And where do they take us?"

"I haven't been there yet, Sean." Wasn't much help to him even now, was I? "I don't know."

He sat down on a rock. "It was stupid," he said, "falling out of that tree." He watched the officials take his body into the house. "Done it a million times. Done it drunk, even." He shook his head and laughed. "Fell a million times, too, and nothing but a few bruises. Not once did I break a bone. And now it kills me?" He shook his head. "Stupid."

He paused, sober now. "I had a million warnings, didn't I? Never knew they were warnings till last night." He stood up. "Guess I pushed it too far." He shook his head, smiling. "Always pushing to the limit till I finally got caught." He laughed out loud. "The final catch, that's what this is." He lay down on the grass and closed his eyes. It would be a while before he opened them again.

I sat on the bench studying my son. He had a cynical view of the world, but an even more critical view of himself. How he could step back and see his mistakes so clearly was beyond me. Aware he was out of line, he simply hadn't known the limits. Given enough rope, he kept tugging until he finally hung himself. Do something dangerous often enough and the odds are that eventually, it will get you. Learned all about the laws of chance from Mrs. Harris. Evidently my son hadn't learned it, though—until now.

Unwilling to leave him alone, I stayed to answer his questions after he rested. Vigilance is exhausting, however, and after awhile I succumbed.

When I awoke, Sean was up, dusting himself off. "Something's happening out front," he said, and we walked around to watch the undertakers and an apparently healthy Josh carry his coffin to a waiting hearse. All wore black. "I guess this is it," Sean said.

The procession wound through town to the church cemetery, halting at a newly dug grave. The family, along with many church and townspeople, bowed their heads. Father O'Brien stood at the head of the grave reading a scripture. The flower-covered casket lay next to the pit.

The priest closed the book and said, "Sean O'Malley Burke lived a short, troubled life."

"Got that right," muttered Sean next to me.

Someone sniffled. Kathleen dabbed at her eyes with a hankie. Josh held her hand. Eloise clutched a handkerchief to her nose. Aunt Louise's eyes were red, but Uncle Sean stood tall, his jaw firmly set. The O'Connors appeared dazed—Hugh looked off into the distance, while Mary stared with blank eyes at the coffin. What a sad group.

"His troubles began with the death of his mother, followed by the absence of his father."

No one moved—not Sean, nor I.

"Sean was fortunate to have family members who loved and cared for him as if he were their own son." The crowd nodded. "Kathleen and Josh, his grandparents—Mary and Hugh, his Uncle Sean and Aunt Louise." Sean gazed at each of them as the priest spoke their names.

"But the best these good folk could do was not enough for this one, already distressed when he came to them at the tender age of eight. Sometimes one cannot undo what has been done to a child by that age. He is on a path that cannot be altered."

"Why did you leave us, Dad?" Sean asked while he watched the ceremony.

"There were good times for Sean, times of hope," the priest continued.

Sean listened while I stood next to him, guilty as sin, silent with shame. It was as if this were my judgment day and these my jurors—and the priest? My judge, pronouncing sentence. A sentence my son had paid. "The sins of the fathers'..." *What was it?* "The sins of the fathers shall be visited upon the children...of the third and fourth generation"? I remembered the verse from sermons in Michigan and had thought then of how I suffered because of my own father's wrongdoing. Was the penalty Sean paid not only for my sins but also for my father's, and his before him? Is this how it finally ended, when the youngest, the fourth generation, died out before giving birth to another unlucky generation to follow?

"There was the time Sean played Joseph in the school pageant," said Father O'Brien. "We all hoped the role would rub off on him."

A titter from the group.

"I hated that play," Sean scoffed.

"And when he was in the fourth grade, Sean showed promise with the violin," added the priest. "But playing the violin wasn't popular on the playground, so he put it down."

"Sure as hell wasn't," Sean said. "The guys thought I was a goofball."

"All in all, life was a struggle for young Sean O'Malley Burke, a struggle that is finally over. I say 'finally' as though it has taken a long time. To us, fifteen seems much too early for this one to be gone, yet for him who had to endure, it must've seemed an eternity."

"So he's saying I was doomed to turn out this way, and it's just as well my life's over? Is that what he's saying? That I never would've amounted to much anyway?"

His voice rose as he walked up to the priest. "Is that what you're saying?" He shouted at everyone now, yelling his frustration at the top of his lungs. "I was no good, so it's just as well I'm gone?"

But none of them could hear him.

"You stupid people! Damn you! Then condemn every one of my buddies to death, too, because they were in it as much as I was. Could have been them just as easily. How come I'm dead and not them? Huh? Answer me that one!" he demanded, then turned to me—the one witness to his tirade—and pointed. "You!"

I stood mute.

"You!" he shouted again, moving toward me.

I backed away, a coward after all.

"Why did you leave?" he demanded, his face breaking up into tears now. "We needed you," he lamented. "Why did you leave us, Dad?"

I had no answer. No excuse. I shrugged and shook my head ever so slightly.

And then, the sky grew very, very bright.

Oh no, I thought.

As Sean watched the sky open and the brilliance unfold—his anger transformed into awe. Then he smiled, and I beheld upon his face great joy. Something in the brilliance beckoned, and he moved up into the light, forgetting me, the crowd and his anger, until the radiance enfolded him so completely, I could no longer see him. Gently but swiftly, just as it had unfolded, the sky closed, and the light faded until it was merely daylight once again.

The crowd, unmoved, watched them lower his coffin into the ground.

Once again, they had come, but not for me.

❖   ❖   ❖

I was unaware of the passing of seasons and changing of weather and light as the sun moved from north to south, back and forth. It all meant so little. My son was dead, gone forevermore. Worse, the lad left believing I had betrayed him.

I didn't understand why they took him but not me. He had been no angel in life, even if it was hard for him in his early days. My own childhood had been troubled, and I had come out of it all right, hadn't I? Thanks in large part to the good people surrounding me. But he had enjoyed the same goodness from the same family and had not responded as well. So why was he taken and I left?

Made me wonder about my father. Was he still walking the planet, like me? To think that some of those I assumed long gone might not be so far away made me uneasy.

"They're as close as you want them to be," said Marnie. Where was she?

"I don't have to be beside you to talk with you."

I shot a thought back at her. *I'm too tired for this, Marnie. No more tricks.*

"I'm not playing tricks. It's the truth. If you know how to do it, the person you're talking to doesn't have to try so hard either," she said. "Try listening to me, but in your mind instead of with your ears, and it will be easier for both of us."

You mean, if I listen to you the way I've talked to you—in my head, that's how it works? Mentally, I listened for an answer. I blocked out the sort of thoughts I usually heard, and waited, listening in what seemed like an empty space inside my mind.

I thought I heard her say, "Exactly," but it could have been my own thinking. "Everybody believes it's their own thinking at first," she clearly said in my mind. "Because it comes to you in your thought, you think you're making it up, but you're not."

Where are you?

"At the cemetery in Ohio. When you talk like this, you don't need to travel 'cross space. Kinda like those telephones they have. You seen them things?"

I've seen 'em. Used one once or twice before I died.

"Well, they talk to each other from long distances over wires like the telegraph, but you hear their real voice the minute they speak. This is like that but without wires or machines. It's just in your head. Telepathy, they call it. And it's real."

I sat, thinking about it.

"Thing is, it's easier for us to do than for the living, but they can do it, too, if they know how to open the space in their heads and listen."

You mean to tell me that living people can hear others in their minds? I shook my head, unbelieving. *Never heard of that.*

"Sure you have. But the ones that did it were supposed to be spiritualists or something like that. Thing is, most anybody can do it. You just don't know it when you're living.

"Ha!" she laughed. "They call them the five physical senses, but what do you call them when ya ain't physical? We still touch, see, hear, smell. What they don't know!" She paused a moment. "Taste is a tough one, though." She was so interested in everything.

But it all seemed pointless to me. *Marnie, I didn't ask you to talk to me.* I pushed my energy out in a bubble and sealed it off.

I thought about what she said though, about feeling your energy like it was a kind of sense. When I was alive, sometimes I sensed when someone was behind me or looking at me. I supposed that was sensing another person's "energy." But I never heard of someone talking to you in your mind.

Then I remembered my inner talks with Mummy. When I was little, I truly believed I heard her voice. But as I grew up and learned such things weren't possible, I passed it off to imagination.

If what Marnie said were true, those talks had been real. Perhaps even the talk with Mrs. Harris outside the pub after she died had been real.

I released my bubble, pulling my energy back in.

Marnie? I asked in my head.

"What?"

It worked!

"Course it works! Unless I have my bubble out," she said, "you can call me any old time. If I'm not clouded up in my own thoughts or busy talking with someone else, I'll hear you."

Do you ever talk with them. . .over there?

"Which over there? The living or the cross-overs?"

The living.

She laughed. "That's my favorite thing to do. But not many of them know they can do it, so it kinda limits who you can talk to." She thought a moment, then said, "I got through to you from far away because it's easier once you're dead."

What about. . .

"Those who crossed over? Depends on what they're doing. You can learn a lot from them, what it's like and stuff like that. Sometimes the one you want to talk with is busy, so someone else comes and speaks for them. But somebody always answers."

The implications were enormous. I might communicate with Susanna, my mother, Mrs. Harris, Maudie, Sean.

"Try it," she said. "Practice. But don't be fooled into thinking it's your imagination when you hear them. It's as real as those people talking to each other on their telephones. Talk to you later."

I had more questions! What about great people like Jesus or the prophets? Could you talk to them? Or historical figures like King Arthur or Abraham Lincoln?

Could you get the living to hear you even if they didn't know it was you? Could you influence them? Imagine the negative aspects if you could make your way into someone's mind without their knowing it. Didn't know if I liked that.

"We do have ethics, you know—well, most of us," and she was gone again.

I got up, then remembered Sean's funeral and sat back down. He had been so angry. I could still hear his cry. "Why did you leave us, Dad?"

Ah, my heart. Why *had* I left? How could I have gone away, never letting them know where I was?

I knew why. Deep inside, I had known that what I did was wrong, wrong, wrong and hid from it like a coward. But after abandoning them, could I go back and say, "Here I am?" They'd demand explanations, and rightly so.

So what had I done? Turned from them completely. Wanted nothing to do with anyone because I didn't want to face their righteous judgment.

But there it was anyway in the face of my son. And in my uncle and Kathleen and Eloise. All of them thought I had done something wrong, whether they said it to my face or not, just like I knew they would. Because they were right.

They were right.

But I had been so devastated over Susanna! The children's faces reminded me so of her! And they had so many needs, so many demands I simply could not live up to. I wasn't good for them, couldn't give them what they needed. Someone else would be better.

Excuses. If I looked inside myself, I knew that what they needed most was for me to stay with them through it all. It had been just as terrible for them as it had been for me. They had lost their mother, for God's sake. If I couldn't identify with that, what kind of person was I?

Then, too, while I had been alive, there had been my own growing awareness that, more and more, I behaved just like my father. I knew what it did to me as a child and hadn't wanted to do that to them.

Underneath all of the excuses for leaving, then, was this: I didn't want to be the father to them that my father had been to me. As a child, wouldn't I have been better off in the hands of good people like Jeremy and Neecie instead of him? Hadn't it been wondrous when Maudie came into my life? And then, when she helped me escape him—well! There can be no argument, can there?

All right, then. Wasn't it better for Sean and Eloise to be with other relatives than with the sour old man I had become? Wasn't this the truth of it?

There it was.

I had done the right thing by them—all of them—whether they knew it or not. I might never be vindicated in their eyes, but in my own heart, I knew I had saved them from a worse life.

It had been the right thing to do after all.

My heart opened and a lightness suddenly filled my being as the weight of my decision to leave lifted off my shoulders. I had done the best thing for my children. I saw it plainly.

Yes, I should have written to explain, but the time for that was past now. They probably wouldn't have understood, anyway. For me, for this moment, it was enough to see and forgive myself.

And forgive myself I did. A deep pit inside me, empty for so long, began to fill, welling up as if to drown me. Unable to restrain it, I began to cry. Face down on my son's grave, clutching the grass in my hands, I cried for all those empty years spent after leaving my children with no family to go home to. I cried for the family life I once had and lost. Even now I couldn't really be with them. I cried because no one but me could understand what I had done. I was so alone. I cried for my own lost childhood and for the loved ones I had lost, those great ladies of my life, gone forever.

What a great sadness.

Much later, finished with my sorrowing, there came inside me an immense peace, a sense of things fitting into place in my life as if there had been some meaning to it. I had enjoyed the love of my life as long as I could, made a good home for her and the children until she died and couldn't do it any longer. I had done right by my Susanna, hadn't I? That was more than some could say.

And I had been a good boy to my mother. Brought her happiness, didn't I? I had done right by Mrs. Harris, too.

I wondered what she would have said to me on this day when I came to a reckoning within myself of all I had done and not done in my life.

I sat up. *Mrs. Harris?* I ventured, clearing a place in my mind for her answer.

You're just kidding yourself, my own voice mocked.

I tried again. *Mrs. Harris, are you there?*

"Aaron, how I have longed to speak with you." My eyes filled again. Sounded like her, but in my head. If those talks with Marnie and my mother were real, this had to be. "It's been hard for you, my dear, hasn't it?"

She knew.

"We can keep up on loved ones from here," she said, "even if you're out of touch with us. We don't exactly watch you. It's more like checking in to find out how things are. We all do that.

"I have seen the terrible things you have gone through and have prayed for you, Aaron."

I love you, Mrs. Harris, I said. My face crumpled just as Sean's had. Ah, me, when would the crying stop?

"And I you, my dear sweet Aaron."

Thank you, Mrs. Harris.

Oh, it was too much. I could talk to her any time! And Susanna, probably, and Mummy!

But I was so so tired.

19

ALONE
Boston, 1946

I came to in the fall. Refreshed, I sat by my son's grave, bringing together in my mind all that had happened since I flew to Boston.

Now I felt as though it were time to leave. But where to go? First needing to see how my family was doing, I glided over to Kathleen's, but it no longer looked the same. Someone had taken off the front gate, and the house was a different color. Entering, I found different furniture and pictures of people I didn't recognize. In the kitchen, a young girl sat at a table eating cookies, her mother pouring milk.

I didn't know these people.

I left and went over to Uncle Sean and Aunt Louise's, which looked as it always had. Some of the older furniture had been replaced within and wallpaper decorated a few rooms, but other than that, it was pretty much the way I remembered.

Someone sang in the kitchen. Aunt Louise. I floated to the doorway and watched as she hummed over a turkey she basted. Pushing it back into the oven, she stood and turned toward the table.

This wasn't Aunt Louise. It was Kathleen, ever so much older, her beautiful red ringlets now gray and pulled back into a knot. Her skin was not as vibrant, but I could see the sparkle still in her eye.

Someone rushed through the door—right through me, in fact. How I hated that! A young girl. "Mmmmm," she said, "smells good!" *Must be Eloise,* I thought. She looked into the glass window of the oven, then turned. Not Eloise at all. "When do we eat?"

Kathleen smiled as she pinched the girl's chin. "Just as I told you before, we eat at four o'clock and not a minute sooner."

"Mama's still in bed." The girl looked to be about fourteen and resembled no one in my family. "I wish she'd do something besides sleep all day."

"Your mother's been through a lot and needs her rest. Why not see if your friends next door are home?"

"Oh, they went to their grandparents' for Thanksgiving. Won't be back till Sunday." She walked to the back door and looked out at the yard. "I wish it would snow. Then at least I could go sledding." She moved to the table and sat down.

Kathleen lifted a bowl of potatoes onto the table. "If you're going to sit there, you'll have to work." The girl picked up the peeler and began on the potatoes.

"When will Mama be better, Kathleen?"

Kathleen talked as she cleaned up the sink. "Oh, it takes time." I had never seen a kitchen like this one, I realized, noticing the gleaming white appliances and copper plumbing, far different from our little farm kitchen in Michigan.

"When I lost Josh, I was down like that for nearly a month till I couldn't bear lying around anymore."

Josh is gone?

She continued washing dishes. "She'll get to the point where she can't stand to be in bed any longer. Then she'll be up and about. You'll see. But today," she turned around, happy, "we're going to get them all up—your mother, my mother, and that no-good father of yours."

The girl sulked again. "Oh, Daddy'll show up for the food. Then he'll go down to the corner to be with his buddies."

"Not on Thanksgiving Day, he won't. They aren't open on holidays."

Someone called from upstairs, but neither of them heard it. "Kathleen!" cried the old voice again.

Oh dear, I thought as I went up and entered the back bedroom. Taking a stick that leaned against the bed, the old woman gave the floor three good whacks. In a moment, the girl appeared at the door.

"Yes, Aunt Louise?"

Now, I was thinking, *if this is Aunt Louise to her, could this be my granddaughter?* If so, then her sick mother would be Eloise! What could have happened to Eloise that would keep her in bed?

"Go down and get Kathleen, Kayla. I need to get up," ordered Aunt Louise. She was very old, this woman who had taken me in as a young boy. Must have been in her eighties at least. I wondered how much longer she had left. Uncle Sean was apparently gone. What about Susanna's parents, were they still around? Not likely.

Kayla—my granddaughter! And Josh died awhile ago? How long had I been out at that graveyard anyway? Sure, the seasons had changed often, but for these people to have aged so, I must have been there a good twenty years or more!

Kathleen entered. "Yes, Mama?"

"Help me get up, dear."

"All right."

Something in Kathleen's tone made her sound very young, taking me back to the first time I had ever seen these two, when Kathleen had helped her mother up after the shock of seeing me at the door. I wondered what kind of a scare it would give old Aunt Louise if she could see me now, and I laughed out loud.

The old woman froze. "What was that?"

Kathleen sat on the bed, pulling her mother's arm across her shoulder, getting ready to stand. "What was what, Mama?"

"That sound, like someone laughing."

She heard my laugh? Shocked, I sat down hard on the bed.

"Will you look at that!" Aunt Louise pointed at me.

"What, Mama?"

"Why, the bed," she said, shaking her finger at me. "The edge just went down all by itself."

Kathleen looked at the spot where I sat.

I didn't dare move.

"I don't remember it being like that."

"Just happened. I saw it go down, just now."

"Now, Mama, it didn't move by itself."

"Sure did. Saw it with my own two eyes."

Both looked at the spot where I sat on the bed. I had sat on many things and no one ever noticed before. Why now? I thought about how I had laughed. Impulsively, with a lot of energy. And I sat down the same way.

That was it! Throwing the pen at the undertaker's had been impulsive, and took energy to do it. But later, when I tried to pick it up, my hands went right through it. So, if I did something with a lot of energy, I could affect their layer!

"I'm telling you, it moved," said Aunt Louise, still pointing at the bed. "Isn't my eyes playing tricks either." She turned to Kathleen, sad now. "Kathleen, why don't you believe me anymore?"

Kathleen looked at her mother. "Mama, I believe you saw it happen."

Now was my chance. I slowly rose from the bed and it resumed its normal shape.

Kathleen looked at it. "Well, isn't that the strangest thing."

"There now," said Aunt Louise, satisfied. "Didn't I tell you?"

Kathleen ran her hand over the blanket. "I don't understand." She walked to the door and sighed. "There's so much we just don't know."

Amen to that.

She shook her head and left the room.

I soon learned that Eloise was recovering from a missed pregnancy, one of several. Her husband, a down-and-out drunk, held no job nor had other family. Getting Eloise with child seemed to be the only thing he could accomplish, but that was no good either. Out of six pregnancies, the only one she kept was Kayla, her first. In spite of the doctor's warnings, Hal—his name was— kept selfishly at her. Each miss left her less of a woman in her own eyes and further weakened, physically.

They all lived in the house with Aunt Louise, and Kathleen cared for everyone. What a mess, I thought. This family had been so healthy. Now look at them.

Where were Kathleen's siblings? Why weren't they helping? Ah, no matter. She had always been the one to make things better. No surprise that she took care of everybody now. Even my no-account son-in-law.

Kayla appeared healthy enough with a normal attitude for her age, given the situation. Perhaps one of my offspring would turn out all right.

I wondered why Eloise chose a drunk for a husband, then realized with a catch that my mother had done the same, and she had been a pearl. Had a big heart, did my mother. Didn't want to see the bad in anyone, which was her undoing of course. She most probably blinded herself to my father's faults when they were courting, the blindfold coming off too late.

Eloise stayed bedridden even after Kathleen's foreseen month passed. I watched as she lay sleeping or looking out the window without seeing, lost in herself. Knew how that felt. Plenty were the days I sat in front of a window those first long winters in Michigan after Susanna's death. Eloise was not unlike her tragic mother, either. What was this melancholy that abounded so in the ones I loved—my mother, Susanna and now Eloise?

What was happening inside her now? Was she overwhelmed? Her baby sister and mother dead, abandoned by her father, Josh gone, her husband ending up the way he was, not to mention her miscarriages—all had taken their toll and left this shell of a woman who appeared to be fading away. Those symptoms, I recognized.

"Oh, Mama," entreated Kayla a week before Christmas as I observed from a chair in the bedroom. "Come downstairs and see the tree." Eloise didn't respond, so Kayla turned from pleading to cheerful. "It's so beautiful, Mama! Kathleen and I decorated it ourselves. We even made popcorn and cranberry strings."

A smile played around Eloise's lips. Kayla, too young to understand the mother-love that forces itself to comfort others through one's own pain, was encouraged and prattled on. "We got out Josh and Kathleen's old ornaments. Remember them? You painted some yourself."

Was there something I could do to help my daughter, I wondered? Could she hear if I spoke to her telepathically?

Eloise, I tried, while Kayla continued to chatter. *Eloise, can you hear me?*

She rolled over to face me, her eyes still closed, the slightest hint of a smile on her lips. Had she heard?

Eloise, what's the matter?

Silence. Then, "Daddy?" Her lips were still, but I heard her voice clear as day in my head. Kayla chattered on.

Eloise. Yes it's me, your father.

"I don't feel good, Daddy."

I know, sweetheart. I know you don't feel good. Extraordinary. Was this really happening, or was it all my imagination? I decided to believe it was real. *Tell me what's wrong.*

"I don't know, Daddy. I feel all mixed up inside. I'm so tired, I can't even talk." Her voice faded off.

"Oh, Mama, I wish you'd get up," Kayla mourned. Her mother lay unresponsive.

I'm here, Eloise. Rest now. We'll talk more later.

"Yes. Rest." Still, her lips did not move, nor could Kayla know we conversed while she talked to her dormant mother. Then, "Is it really you, Daddy?" She sounded so young.

Yes, it's me, Eloise.

Drowsy now. "I missed you." Even Kayla saw the smile.

Eloise fell asleep, and Kayla tiptoed out of the room. "I think she's better," she whispered to Kathleen who had come to the door to see what was going on.

Eloise *was* better in one sense. Color came back to her face, and later that evening she ate a little for supper. I believed that my communication might have helped.

That night, Hal came home stinking of drink and mounted the stairs to the garret. Shades of my father, he attempted to rouse Eloise from her sleep. He went about it quietly, for fear of waking the others, no doubt. But he did his damage nonetheless.

Eloise submitted. I sensed her shame if the others were to know how bad this really was. I watched him push her around, pain growing in me. The woman was ill! How could he treat her like that?

I could not let this go on. Furious, I picked up a candlestick, lunged forward and hit him with it.

"Ouch!" he yelled, gaping first at the floor where the candlestick fell, then at the spot on the bedstand where it had sat a moment before.

Fueled with anger, I kicked him.

"Ow!" He cursed, jumping up. "What is this?" Drunk he was and not trusting his own mind, so I let him have it again, punching him hard in the stomach. He doubled over, fell and passed out.

Serves you right, I thought.

He moved out the next day. Said the place was haunted, and I guess it was. The rest of the family was relieved he was gone, but Eloise took a turn for the worse.

"Why'd he leave me?" she cried, coming out of her stupor. The family thought this might be progress, but I was alarmed. Had my actions done her even more harm? "Everyone leaves me, everyone," she sobbed.

Ach! There it was again.

She cried, then quieted and said, "You know, even though I hardly remember her, I think Mama died because she didn't want to stay with us."

Kayla stood at the end of the bed, wiping her eyes with a hankie.

"I'm sorry, Kayla," Eloise said.

"What for, Mama?"

"For making your daddy go away." Her eyes brimmed again.

Oh my God. She blamed herself for Kayla's lack of a father now.

"Mama," Kayla moved to the bedside, "he isn't good. He was mean to you and didn't want me around."

Eloise nodded. "My father was the same with me."

I grimaced but wasn't going to turn away this time. Eloise needed her father now, though she knew it not, and I wasn't about to leave, no matter what anyone said or felt about me.

Reaching up, she smoothed Kayla's hair. "I chose your daddy, and I don't regret it. I wouldn't have you if I hadn't married him. I'm just sorry it didn't work out." Kayla lay her head on her mother's breast.

Eloise fell back into her silent world the next day and never spoke again. I stayed with her in the corner chair for three months while she died. Several times, she separated from her comatose physical body, rising above it. Once, she moved to where I sat, looked at me and smiled, then returned to bed.

When the Grand Moment came, she lifted out of her body and came to stand beside it. Though not new to this state, I don't believe she realized the difference. This time, she was dead.

"I think I'm better," she said in a dreamy voice.

"Perhaps so," I responded.

Her dreamy gaze found me. Her eyes focused, then widened. "Daddy?" she asked, her voice higher now. "Daddy? Is it you?"

I thought she'd remember, but apparently she didn't. "'Tis me, Eloise."

She looked at me quizzically. "I missed you, Daddy."

"I know, little one." I hadn't really missed her until I'd been dead awhile, had I?

Troubled, she watched family members approach the bedside, crying aloud. "Why don't they see that I'm better?"

"Because you've left them, and they're sad."

She stiffened. "Do you mean that . . . I'm dead?"

"Eloise, what's 'dead' to them and what death really is are two different things." She looked confused. I found a simpler explanation. "But yes, you died today and are here with me now."

"But why can't I be with them? They love me." She watched as Kayla, at the bedside, kissed her mother's cheek. "Oh, Kayla! My dear, sweet, baby girl. How I failed you," she cried and ran to Kayla, attempting a hug, but her arms went right through her daughter. Eloise jumped back, horrified.

"She can't hear you, Eloise. Can't see you either. They don't know you're still here." I said it slowly so she could digest the meaning. "We can see and hear them, but we can't really touch them."

"NO!" she screamed, running to Kathleen on the other side of the bed. "Kathleen! Kathleen, look at me," she cried as Kathleen pulled the coverlet over the body's face.

She turned to me. "You're wrong! I'm right here."

The family left the room. The candle beside the bed flickered as the door closed. We were alone, just Eloise and me. She sat down heavily on a chair and stared at the covered body.

Wishing to help her through this, I walked to her side and stooped next to her, putting my arm across her shoulder, but she threw it off and stood up, knocking me off balance.

"Get *away* from me." She moved to the other side of the room.

Shaken, I regained my footing. "I understand," I said. And I did.

"If you had stayed after Mamma died," she began, "maybe I would've grown up to take care of my own baby better. Maybe I wouldn't have chosen such a horrible husband." She looked at me, malice growing in her narrowing eyes. "He was so like you."

What? I had not been a drunk, had been a good provider for my children, had even left them all that money when I could no longer...

"You were never nice and didn't do anything with either of us." She walked back and forth around the bed. "He left me, you know," she said, "just like you did."

"Eloise," I began.

"No!"

"I couldn't take care of you and was no good for you."

"Be quiet!" She ran at me and pounded my chest with her fists. I didn't protect myself as she hit me and hit me until she tired, then collapsed in a heap, sobbing.

I sat down next to her. "Maudie did the right thing, sending you to Boston. I never could've done for you what they did."

"Why not?"

Ah, that was the question now, wasn't it?

"I don't know," I admitted. "After your mother passed, there was nothing left in me for anyone, including myself."

She lay awhile, head on the floor, her eyes open. "But you came back for this—for me—didn't you?" she said, almost to herself. "How long have you been like—this?" She gestured to herself, then me.

"Must be twenty years or more."

She was silent a spell. "We didn't know what happened."

"I know," I said. "I'm sorry."

She lay back. I lifted her and carried her to the overstuffed chair in the corner where I had spent the past three months and set her down.

She looked up at me again—but this time it was different. Her eyes were clear, almost shining. "Thank you Daddy," she said. "Thank you for being here for me now."

And then, an expression of surprise crossed her face, followed by a look of wonder, and she disappeared. No sky opened, no bright light unfolded. Nothing. She simply vanished.

I looked at the bed. Her body was gone.

I hurried to the cemetery, where the crowd at the grave was already dispersing. How had I missed it? Why did time pass so differently when one was entirely in the Second Layer? Here I had labored to stay in the physical time frame all through her illness. It had been tiring, but I had done it. Once we were both in the Second Layer though, days passed like minutes.

Where had she gone?

"Eloise!" I called out. I turned in another direction. "Eloise!"

No answer.

Eloise! I called telepathically, clearing a place in my thoughts for her reply, but none came. I began to run, looking for her in the cemetery. Frantic, I shouted again. "Eloise!"

"Daddy, it's so beautiful!" The answer came in my mind.

I stopped. *Where are you?*

"They're here, Daddy, all of them. Mama and Sean, and... just everyone! Didn't you see them?"

I was stunned. How could this grand and glorious event occur right where I was, and I not witness it?

"Oh," she said, sad now. "They tell me you weren't supposed to see."

But why Eloise?

A moment's delay. She seemed to be asking and receiving an answer from someone. I could hear none of it, just had the sensation that was what must be happening.

"They say that if you had seen it, you might have come, too," she said, clearly unhappy now. "Oh, Daddy, I'm so sorry. They say I had to leave without you."

She was gone.

Of all the horrendous events, this had to be the worst. I had found her. Spoken with her. Dedicated myself to staying with her as she died, never once leaving her side, bound and determined never to abandon her again. And even though she didn't understand why I left her in life, she hadn't rejected me as completely as Sean had. And she had been taken from me anyway.

I was alone once more.

Oh, the sorrow of it. I cannot bear to think on the time I mourned her departure. My little girl had been right with me. She had needed me to be a good father to her, and I *had* been, at the end. Even so, she had been forced to leave—all right—to *abandon* me.

As I look on it now and see the beauty of it all, it seems as if the time that passed after Eloise left was as the blink of an eye, so swiftly does it all go by. But immersed in the experience, it seemed to go ever so slowly.

After spending an interminable period in her cemetery, it occurred to me that I might be alone for all time. They were all gone now—Susanna; my beautiful, though troubled, children;

Maudie; and the rest. I saw upon walking the family plot that Aunt Louise now rested beside Uncle Sean, Kathleen next to Josh. Kayla, I didn't see. Having no idea how much time had passed and not wishing to know more, I never searched for her. If my father still roamed the earth, I didn't want to know that either. Never wanted to see him again.

Yes, I could speak with them in my mind if I tried. Sure I could. But I wanted to see them, to feel my arms around each of them, to sit and laugh and cry and talk and explain what had happened and why I'd done what I had. And I couldn't.

I was condemned to be alone.

Oh, I could see the dark humor in it. That I, who had wanted little to do with people should wish so desperately for their company now, was a tragic joke. Perhaps it was what I deserved. Perhaps a form of justice. I didn't know about any of that. I would never see them again, that I did know. And to care about anything more was beyond my ken.

I watched the living come from time to time, burying their dead or visiting those already entombed. Other sad souls like me lolled about. None of them wished to be bothered, and neither did I. We all had our problems. And we all wanted to be left alone.

It was comical, in a way. I wished to be with those of my choosing, but not those already around me. Mournful that I had been left behind, I thought myself alone, yet I wasn't, really. Any number of times, I could have had company, if I had gone out of myself and spoken with one of these distressed beings. But although lonesome, I chose to be solitary rather than speak to any of them.

It was a strange paradox, if you will, and I paused in my suffering to reflect upon it for some time, coming to the conclusion that either I wanted to be alone . . . or I didn't. Deciding on the latter, I roused myself and strolled the cemetery. Seeing few beings I would relish spending even a moment with, I thought back to my own cemetery in Ohio.

I wondered how she was faring.

Marnie, I called.

Silence. Perhaps she was in her bubble.

Marnie, I called again, but she didn't answer. When she didn't respond after several days, I resolved to see her again. Kneeling at the grave of each loved one, I said goodbye and, turning southwest, headed for Ohio.

It was not the best weather for flying. Harsh winds hindered swift movement, and the trip took much longer and used more energy than I thought I had in me.

Finally though, I reached the outskirts of the town where I had been buried. So many changes had taken place over the decades. Automobiles instead of horses and carriages filled the widened streets. Houses abounded, and older buildings had been replaced with new ones.

I located the old cemetery in the middle of town, flew over the gates and set down once again at the only spot on earth I could truly say belonged to me.

'Tis a strange experience to look upon one's grave and see your own headstone. I had been unknown in this town, and the stone was small and primitive. Yet my name was there and the date I had died:

AARON BURKE

d. August 8, 1922

How much time had passed since my remains had been laid to

rest? What condition were they in now? A skeleton would be all, I supposed.

I was tired, but not too tired to look for Marnie. I moved closer to her grave. She wasn't there. Searching the cemetery, I didn't see her at all.

I did see the old guy by Esther Fielding's grave. Walking over, I stood beside him, not caring whether I incurred his wrath or not. "Mr. Fielding," I said. He didn't move. "Mr. Fielding!" I shouted.

He turned slowly to look up at me. "Oh," he said. "You," and turned back to look at her stone.

"Mr. Fielding," I said, "where's Marnie?"

He ignored me. I tried again. Finally, he turned, irritated. "Who?"

I pointed to her gravestone. "The . . ." I was going to say "whore" but remembered she hadn't thought of herself that way. "The girl whose grave is right there."

"Oh," he said. " The whore."

Submitting, I nodded.

"Gone," he said, again turning to face the stone.

"Where'd she go?"

"Gone, I said. You deef? Where do any of them go? You tell me that. I'd like to know." He pointed to his wife's headstone. "Her, too." Bowing his head, he mumbled, "Then maybe I can get there."

They had come for Marnie. That's why I hadn't heard from her in so long. Sure, I could turn to her in my mind, but I had so wanted to see the only friend I could still lay eyes on.

For the first time, I studied Mr. Fielding. The man really didn't want anything more than I did—simply to be with his wife, his loved one. We were the same, weren't we? Just cut out a little differently, each of us. I felt the beginnings of empathy for this man. I was tired, but this feeling was something new, and it seemed to give me some spirit.

"Did you see her go?" I indicated Marnie's stone.

He paused. I could feel the question inside him. *Why doesn't he go away?* he wondered. I knew how he felt but needed to talk with him. "Yes, I saw her go," he said.

"Well, what was it like?"

"Say," he turned to face me, angry at being interrupted, more angry at being asked to speak his pain. "What is it to you, anyhow? You don't care."

"I want to know if it was like what I've seen."

"Seen one, you've seen them all," he said, dismissing me.

I was not to be put off. "So why do you stay by your wife's grave? She's already gone, isn't she?"

"You know, you're becoming a real pain in the ass."

I had to agree but pushed on. "Mr. Fielding," I said, "I miss my wife, too. I want to know why you stay by your wife's grave if she's already gone."

He sighed, turned and looked up at me. "Look," he began, "it's like this."

I sat down. Something big was coming. I could feel it.

"Sometimes," he said, "they'll come back for you." He looked at her stone again. "Seen it happen." He gestured to the eastern end of the cemetery, "Watched another old guy over there do it."

I looked and saw some old stones but no one by them.

"Stayed by her grave for years. I talked to him some but could see he just wanted to be left alone." He looked up. "Kinda like me."

I nodded but wasn't going away until I knew what he had to say.

"Said that if you think on that one special person, and think over your life, too—maybe even pray about it—that sometimes," he looked at me, a warning in his eye, "sometimes, mind you, they come back for you."

I gasped and opened my mouth to speak, but he motioned me to be quiet till he was done.

"Doesn't always happen," he said. "Look at me. I'm still here. Been doing this for God knows how long, and it ain't worked. But it worked for him." He waved east again. "Don't see anyone over there, now, do you?"

I shook my head.

"Told me before he went that he'd been doing it over fifty years, earth time. Said someone else told him about it. Didn't have anything better to do, so thought he'd give it a try."

Now I had questions. "So you just think about her all the time? Is that how it works? Thinking hard brings her back?"

"Well, it's a little more complicated than that. And sometimes other circumstances get in the way, *if* you know what I mean," he said, indicating me again. "But if you let them know you want them to come back by staying at their grave long enough, some- thing might—it just might—happen." He turned back to her grave. "Now, if you don't mind," he said, terminating the conver- sation.

Oh, God in Heaven, I thought, *please let this be true.* I looked toward Marnie's grave, but it wasn't Marnie I wanted to have come for me.

I knew where I had to be, and it wasn't Ohio either.

❖ ❖ ❖

After a short rest I left, anxious to be at the earthly resting-place of my beloved in the hope that she would come for me. Joyous I was when the little graveyard came into sight. The woods had grown up around it, but I had no trouble finding it. I settled to the ground and saw Maudie's headstone next to her first husband's, Mr. Whitcomb's, and recognized the names of townspeople on others. It was a special cemetery now, dedicated to Civil War veterans buried here. And over there, isolated from the rest, lay my father's grave. I couldn't look, much less visit it.

For me, only one grave lay here. Though little Katy rested next to it, and I recalled her beauty and how Susanna had loved her, Katy's death had brought on her mother's demise. I couldn't quite forget that, though I knew it was not the little one's fault. So I focused upon Susanna. Surely she would come for me.

Lovingly, I gazed upon her headstone. I talked with her out loud and in my head. Sometimes I thought I heard her telepathically, but I couldn't be sure. I wanted to hear her so much, I could be making it up. I thought about what Mrs. Harris did when she was confused and asked God and the angels to help me, leaving it to them—"Thy will be done," and all that.

But never did the sky open for me. Seasons came and went. Winters blew over the cemetery and through me. Each summer, the trees grew taller, and the forest became more dense, hiding the little graveyard from civilization. The living had long ago stopped bringing bodies to this old place. The road grew over until it became simply a path. Trees fell, blocking the way here and there. Relatives visited infrequently. Occasionally, a wandering pedestrian happened upon us and studied with interest the old headstones at this cemetery lost in the forest. Aged wooden crosses marking most of the plots fell apart and decayed.

It began with slight desecrations—a flag gone here, artificial flowers flung there. A small headstone disappeared. Then, older larger stones became trophies for these infidels. It was the final insult to the dead who lay below.

They took the markers belonging to my darlings one at a time. Katy's went first while I stood helpless, enraged at the indignity of it and watched the young thieves carry it off. Then, one hot summer's day, two boys removed the last standing monument to my wife's life. Now, only the sinking of the earth betrayed the grave of my beautiful Susanna.

One snowy winter's night, I conceded that I might remain earthbound forever. This gnawing possibility seemed preposterous at first, for hadn't I seen them come and release the dead? Hadn't I been told that they would come and get you sooner or later? But how much later, and was that for sure? I didn't know the answer, and with no other souls at this cemetery, I couldn't ask anyone.

Another problem. I could no longer communicate in my head. Either I had forgotten how to do it, or I was sealed in my own bubble too well, or—perish the thought—the gift of communication had been rescinded. I called out loud and in my head, but nothing worked. In addition, complete exhaustion made traveling for help unthinkable.

As I thought over the possibilities, casting one out after the other, I finally admitted to myself what was becoming terribly apparent.

I was damned.

I was doomed.

And nothing, and no one, could help me.

20

BREAKTHROUGH
Michigan, 1991

When first the women came, I barely noticed. The cemetery had become more of a curiosity to the living than anything else, and I ignored visitors, choosing to stay in the Second Layer. But the dark-haired woman got my attention when she dropped to her knee in front of Susanna's grave, making the sign of the cross.

Now why, I thought, *would she do that right here when there isn't even a headstone to mark the grave?*

Then she said something bizarre. "Someone's here."

I sat up.

"The hair is standing up on the back of my neck."

Aye, and on the back of mine, too, lady. Could she sense me there?

The other woman paused, looking about. "I feel it, too," she said.

"He's somewhere around here," said the dark one, indicating the very spot on which I sat.

I was dumbfounded. Not one living soul had ever realized I was near. Was it possible that someone living could actually feel my presence and know I was here?

They stayed a few minutes, then turned to go.

I didn't understand. If they knew I was there, why wouldn't they stay longer to explore?

"Come on, boys," said the light-haired woman to the children who tagged along. "It's getting dark."

Ah. Twilight it is, and not the place to be after hours, I thought as they filed down the path away from me.

No. I could not allow this. Desperate, I called out. "Don't leave!"

Last in line, the light-haired woman turned and looked straight through me.

"Don't go," I pleaded.

Her group disappearing into the darkening forest, she ran to catch up with them. "Wait up, you guys!" she shouted.

"Don't leave me," I called, forlorn. But she was gone.

To have someone actually recognize I was here—what could this mean? And hadn't it been something when the first one knelt before this very grave! What a kindness for her to bless this place in such a way, bringing me to think on the spiritual beliefs and practices that lent some comfort in life. I pondered upon this for a time but wound up wondering where the gracious Deity was now and His Son who had promised redemption.

I wasn't ready when the light-haired woman came the second time. She brought others and spoke again of "feeling" someone there. The children giggled. Aye, a joke it was in fact, but on me you see—a nasty, cruel joke, and I contemplated that for a time, too.

By her third visit, I had put to rest my anger at being abandoned, for was I truly deserted if this one kept coming back to me? It was me she came to see, mind you. Though a year or two may have passed between visits, each time she came she spoke of feeling a "presence." That had to mean me.

And so I awakened from my reverie the third time she walked into my experience. Twilight again it was, and soon after arriving, she rounded up her children to leave. But she lingered and looked back.

I had long ago determined that this time would be different. "Don't go!" I shouted with all my might.

She stopped completely and turned, a quizzical expression of—could it be empathy?—on her face, appearing to make a decision. And nothing would ever be the same.

I will never forget her words.

"Whoever is here..." she called out, then paused.

"I am here!" I answered.

"Whoever is here," she called again, "my heart is with you!" She was the first living person to speak to me in nearly a century.

Old Man Fielding's words of yore rang in my head. "If you're desperate enough, you'll find a way." There was no time to think, to weigh the consequences. I followed, leaving behind Susanna's remains and any further possibility of her coming for me at the cemetery. I followed them, for the prospect of staying in that place any longer was more than I could bear.

This single impulse would alter the remainder of my earthly existence.

We moved quickly through the woods, for it was getting dark. The light-haired woman caught up with the others.

"That was corny," she said.

"What was?" asked a woman ahead.

"What I just said. What does it mean, anyway—'My heart is with you'?"

"It means you care."

"Yes," she agreed, "I care."

Ah, little lady, thank you for caring, I thought as I followed her out of the woods. I believe she felt me behind her for she looked back several times as we made our way. Didn't see me though. No flash of recognition showed on her face as it would have had she seen me.

We reached a vehicle parked at the path's end. The other woman pushed a button on a key that opened all the doors. Everyone piled in, two in front, three in the rear, no room for me. I threw myself across their legs in back as the doors closed. Straightening, I squeezed in. The driver started the engine, moved a stick, and we advanced. Swiftly.

My lady inspected the inside of the vehicle. "What if he's in here?"

I was there! She must know that.

"He couldn't be," said little Evan. "Where would he sit?"

Indeed.

"He's a ghost," she said. "He doesn't need space."

She was wrong in that. I did need space. Compromising my energy with these strangers in their slower, thicker layer by over-lapping our bodies was uncomfortable as could be.

We moved at an alarming rate. I looked out the window in fright. Certainly, we must have gone this fast on the train, but this vehicle was so small, I was sure that any minute we would careen off the road and…what? We all die?

Oh, embarking on such a wild adventure was not to my liking, but to be called by this visitor was something I could not ignore. I couldn't let her get away. It was out of the question.

In a moment, we did turn toward a tree. I cringed, waiting for the impact, but then we were on a side road—actually, a private lane. *Oh, my.* Down a hill, then up. Slowing now, thanks be to God, and then we stopped.

I looked out at a little yellow cottage about the size of our old farmhouse. Quaint it was, with flowers growing by the door. But I hadn't long to tarry. The others were already out of the auto, and I slipped out just before the door slammed. Didn't like to go through doors if I didn't have to.

The cottage was located on the Big Lake. When I had last visited the shore, nothing but nature had been here. Now, cabins and cottages lined the beach. As we entered, I noticed strange gadgets in the kitchen. But then, the basics were still there—a roof over our heads, furniture-filled rooms, places to sleep. Some things didn't change.

Taking a peripheral notice of this, I focused on getting my lady's attention. I had it at the cemetery, but now they spoke of me no more. She must have dismissed the possibility I might be around, which distressed me. I was so tired, I couldn't stay in their layer much longer. I had to find a way to show I was still with her!

The three women and their sons sat in the parlor conversing, laughing, enjoying each other's company. Soon, it was time for bed, and they withdrew to their rooms.

I followed her. "Linda," they'd called her. She got into bed and put the light out. My opportunities waned! She would fall asleep if I didn't do something now.

The pencil. Throwing the pencil. Throwing that candlestick at Hal. Punching him. I could do it then. I had to do it now. Desperation fueling me, I exploded into a kick at the foot of her bed.

She sat straight up.

Aha! Felt it, she did. Gleefully I waited, but after a while she lay back down.

Maybe I hadn't done it hard enough. *All right then.* I kicked it again. Surprised myself with that one, I must say. Didn't know I had it in me.

Sat bolt upright she did, looking around. She turned on the lamp, crawled to the end of the bed and examined the very spot where I'd done the deed. She sat up for quite some time. Finally, though, she did lie down but her eyes stayed wide open.

Perhaps if I yelled. "Lady!"

She tossed and turned.

"LADY! I'm talking to you!"

But she didn't respond. If she didn't connect the kick with me now, would she tomorrow, as the memory of the cemetery faded even more? How could I make her realize I was here?

Breaking through dimensions takes energy, and I with so little to begin with, had to rest. Sitting on the floor at the foot of her bed, I buried my head in my arms. *I'll rest,* I told myself...*for just a moment.*

Morning came and with it, many activities. The ladies wanted to "gift shop." Linda, almost as tired as I, agreed to accompany them. Myself? I knew that if I didn't get through to her today, it might never happen. But I could hardly move, so I stayed at the house in my own layer.

Soon, the auto came up the drive, and Linda got out, complaining of weariness. "I'm sorry, you guys. I've got to take a nap. Didn't sleep too well last night." They went on without her and she entered the house and headed straight for the bedroom.

She lay down on the bed. Now was my chance. I had to move fast but didn't want to scare her, merely get her attention. I thought of sitting on Aunt Louise's bed and sped to the side Linda lay facing—her eyes open, thinking. I leaned over and placed my fists on the mattress. Using every bit of energy I could muster, I pushed the mattress down in front of her face, then slowly released it.

Her eyes opened wide. She sat straight up, swinging her feet to the other side of the bed, her back to me.

"You're here!" she cried.

Jesus, Mary and Joseph! I had done it.

She took a deep breath. "Okay," she said, her voice shaky. It had to be a shock, after all. What would she be thinking? That the house is haunted? That she wanted me out of here? Did she want to scream and call for help?

None of these. She became very calm. "I can help you," she said.

Dear Father in Heaven. How could she help me, when I—who had been in this state for decades—didn't know how to help myself? True, she had known to call to me at the cemetery, although she hadn't quite put it together when I kicked her bed, had she?

"I know someone who can help you get to Heaven and be with your loved ones."

Dear God. Could they call Susanna? It was too much to hope for.

"But," she said.

I looked up. It *was* too good to be true.

"You have to agree not to scare me anymore. No kicking the bed, no more bumps in the night, no tricks."

Oh, I could agree to that. Moving things in the Physical wearied me. Just staying in their layer tired me altogether, but I would do it. Besides, I had no need to play more tricks. I had her attention now.

"My friend lives in Arizona. I live there, too. We leave on Friday."

Arizona? But that was so far away! Would she bring this woman back?

Friday, she just said. *What day is today?* I wondered.

"Today is Wednesday. You can come with me."

"Oh, I don't think so, little one. I simply don't have the energy for such a journey." Disheartened, I sank back against the wall.

"Don't worry. I'll tell you what to expect ahead of time so you'll know what to do. But, please. We have to do this my way."

That I would do. "You, my friend, are taking me into an unfamiliar world where I wouldn't *know* what to do. I will surely do my best to stay with you."

"We fly to Arizona on Sunday."

"Fly?" The living couldn't fly. It would take weeks for me to fly there, depending on the weather. All the way to Arizona . . . I began to have serious doubts about the possibilities with this one, after all.

"So," she said, beginning to plan, "my sister-in-law arrives Thursday. She'll be in a white van."

"A van?"

"It's a motor vehicle, like a car, but larger, longer, more rectangular. She'll take us Friday and drop us off at my parent's house, just outside of Detroit. Then on Sunday, my folks will take us to the airport. You'll get out with me there."

"Airport?" What about her children?

"The boys will stay at my parents' house until their father flies in to get them."

All this flying! I didn't know they could do it.

"You and I will change planes in St. Louis and we'll arrive in

Arizona later that same day."

We could get to Arizona in one day?

Change planes? What did that mean? A plane was a flat surface. How could we change from one plane to another? Was it like changing from the Physical to the Second Layer and back?

"You don't know about planes and things like that, do you?"

I shook my head. Silly, when she couldn't see me.

"Have you seen those machines with wings that fly in the sky?"

Oh, I had noticed them. The first time I saw one, it pulled me right out of a reverie, so surprising was the sight. Yes, I had seen sky machines many a time.

"Those are planes; airplanes. They carry people and their luggage all over the world."

Oh. She wanted me to ride in a sky machine. I recollected hearing of fools experimenting with them in my lifetime but had discounted the stories. Apparently, "flying" had become common.

Then I realized something new. She answered my thoughts. This woman could hear me in her head! Tremendous!

From that point on, whenever Linda and I were alone, she asked questions aloud, and I answered. But she didn't always hear me correctly.

"What's your name?" she asked, still sitting on the bed.

Aaron, I answered in my head.

"Eh —, Eh —?"

"Aaron," I said out loud this time.

"Oh. Edward."

"No, not Edward. AARON!" I shouted. "For God's sake, not Edward. That's my father's name." Now how had she connected me with that, of all names? Both started with vowels, but the rest? Had she somehow linked my father with me?

"All right, Edward," she said, pleased.

Oh no, I thought. To be recognized as Edward over the following days would be poetic justice. The fruit fell not far from the tree after all. I smiled. Once again, the joke was on me.

Linda described every step of our journey before it happened, and each occurred just as she said it would, except for one that would wreak havoc when it fell through. It never occurred to me that everything wouldn't happen exactly as planned. She seemed so self-assured, so capable. She knew people who worked with ghosts, for God's sake! How often did one run into that? I had to trust her. Besides, what were the alternatives?

The truth of it was that, however imperfect, our communication was my sole connection now to any other being, physical or not. I enjoyed the sense of companionship and believe she did, too. The room vibrated with excitement.

As exhilarating as it must have been for her, never once did she mention my existence to anyone while we were in Michigan. Perhaps she was afraid of scaring them or that they might think her a little off. Whatever her reasons, I was glad she kept it between us. It was as if she were protecting me. A long time it had been since anyone had cared for me enough to do that, and it felt infinitely good.

The ladies returned later that afternoon with the boys. Linda never got her nap, but, energized by our encounter, she didn't seem to need it.

That evening they had a rollicking time reminiscing. Never knowing when she might leave the room, I stayed vigilant and listened in, smiling, even laughing with them, forgetting my exhaustion. What a blessing to be freed even momentarily from such suffering. When was the last time I enjoyed myself like this?

I don't know why she began to confide in me. Perhaps she sensed things cross my mind that I didn't fully understand—or possibly even accept—about her ways. For example: that first night as she readied herself for bed, she endeavored to explain the circumstances that left her a single woman with children.

"I'm divorced," she whispered. She always spoke aloud to me, albeit not quite so loudly now, since others in the house might wonder who she talked to. The extraordinary thing was that she heard me in her head. I couldn't get over that, though Marnie had said some could do it.

"So many people are divorced today. It's terrible when a marriage fails. So hard to give up, move out, start over again. So difficult for the children." She sighed. "They say half the marriages now end in divorce, Edward."

"Half? What a tragedy."

"I know it wasn't like that when you were alive." She was apologizing for her culture! "You stayed with your families your entire lives, didn't you?"

"Some did, some didn't. But not I, little one," said I, more to myself than to her. I lost my wife—lost my life for that matter—when she died. And then, for all intents and purposes, had to abandon my children. It's true that others remained married, and many times not for the better, if you think on it. Look at Mummy. She would have been better off without my father. Maudie, too.

No, not many divorced. Some of us simply deserted our families in one way or another when we couldn't or didn't want to put up with them any longer. At least with divorce, there was the decency of notification.

"Well," Linda said, "is it better to stay in a bad marriage or move on? And then the question is, move on to what? I haven't married again, and my children suffer because their father and I are apart."

"My children suffered, too, little one, because I left them. You at least have yours with you."

"But when they're with me, they aren't with their father," she answered. "They never have us both at the same time." Then she laughed. "Of course, when we *were* all together, it was a disaster. So maybe it's just as well."

The next day, her friends left, and Linda finished cleaning and packing. I had forgotten how much labor staying alive entailed. Here in the Second Layer, you did not work to survive. You simply *were*. But the living had to work. She washed and dried clothing and bedding in large square machines. How much easier than the old washboard, ringer and clothesline! And there was much cleaning of the place. Imagine! A machine that sucked dirt off the floor and out of the carpets. Astonishingly noisy. Even so, I wondered if the rugs didn't still need a good beating out-of-doors.

Thursday, Carol—the sister-in-law in the white van—arrived. The next day, we packed ourselves into it. Off we went at a terrifying speed—away from the cemetery, away from the farm and its memories, away from things all too familiar—to an unknown place I had never cared to see and didn't wish to visit.

But what was I going to do, stay here another hundred years?

21

FLYING HOME
Michigan, 1995

Adventure was in the air. Linda's family and I headed "downstate" in the van. How exhilarating to observe the world fly by. And all the billboards! I saw one asking, "Have a problem with gambling?" followed by another saying, "Win big at the casino!" They became brash! Shocking, even! One for a place called "Hooters!" followed by, "Having problems conceiving?"

Things had changed, and some not for the better. Certainly modes of transportation had improved. But concrete cities replaced the towns and villages of yesteryear. I was shocked when we passed through Flint—a booming town when I lived there. Dead weeds surrounded abandoned factories now. Outside the cities, huge tracts of farmland grew single crops that must deplete the soil. And where were all the forests? Had the loggers come this far south? What had we humans done?

Linda sat in front, conversing with Carol. She couldn't talk to me with people around, so I couldn't ask my questions. I grew tired and closed my eyes.

Upon our arrival, Linda's father unloaded the baggage and

parked me in a garage. Linda and I had agreed that I would stay in the van. No point haunting another house.

I settled in and waited. Each time her father came out, I thought, *This is it!* But instead, we went on several short jaunts to the post office, a bank and a hardware store. The latter greatly interested me. I was tempted to explore it, but what if he left without me? I remained in the van.

On Sunday, we left for the airport and entered a building of metal and glass, people rushing hither and thither below a towering ceiling. So many were the signs, one would have to know which to look for. Piercing voices echoed throughout announcing flights, calling names, giving instructions.

Linda handed her bags to a porter who designated a "gate," and we hiked a good ways, stopping at a checkpoint where people walked through a small frame.

"It's a weapons detector," she whispered. They still had guns, then.

We reached our gate—really a holding pen with seats for travelers.

"In a few minutes, we can board," she said, but her lips didn't move. She said it telepathically! Wonderful! Now we could converse anytime!

A voice called rows thirty to thirty-nine, then twenty to thirty.

"It won't be long now, Edward. Stay with me."

Indeed, I will, little one. Wouldn't let you out of my sight if my soul depended on it. Which it did.

"Now boarding rows ten to twenty."

"Here we go." She rose, gathered her baggage and strode for the open door. Following meant overlapping myself with others as we crowded down the enclosed gangway that turned at the end. I crossed a threshold and boarded a cabin more cramped than the holding pen. She searched for her row with me close behind, sat down and buckled a belt across her hips.

Immediately, a man steamed through me to a row farther back. More approached. This was not good. The ceiling too low for me to lift overhead, I began to panic.

"Edward," she said, "You don't have to stay right beside me. Go find a spot to sit. When we land, come back."

I backed up until I could go no farther, leaning against the rear of the cabin, barely able to see my lady halfway forward.

Suddenly, the engines roared, vibrating the very fabric of the plane. We backed away and turned, moved ahead and turned again. Then a crescendo of noise, and the plane accelerated down the runway until the front tipped up, and the earth fell away.

I had to see this. Staggering to little oval windows and leaning over the living, I looked out with wonder. *Look at the houses, like tiny squares of confetti! And cars and trucks moving along like little fleas!* I had flown before, but never ever did I imagine flying so high and so fast!

The engines quieted, the plane leveled out, the passengers settled in, and so did I.

We landed frighteningly fast, the engines displaying a final ferocious power that somehow slowed us. I floated to Linda's side as the plane came to a standstill.

We moved up a ramp. "Stay with me, Edward"

I'm right behind you. And it's Aaron.

In the airport now, she walked to a display screen. Then we sped through the crowds. Spoke to me out loud over her shoulder the entire way, she did, even with all the people around.

"Edward," she said as we approached a corner, "get ready. If ever you were to lose me, this is the place."

I could see why. We turned the corner and slammed into a wall of people rushing every which-way, the fear of being late stamped upon their faces. Over the cacophony and clamor of the crowd, disembodied voices echoed their announcements. It was pure pandemonium.

She explained where we were going as we wove through the crowds, then down a smaller hallway to our gate where we boarded. I sat in an empty seat next to Linda, exhausted.

"When this flight ends," she said in her head now, "we'll be in Arizona."

I opened my eyes, and we had already landed. We disembarked and made our way to an area where Linda retrieved her bags, then exited through sliding doors into the hot Phoenix air only to wait at the curb.

"Lisbeth's my best friend," she explained aloud now. "She's the woman who first sensed you at the cemetery. Remember? She kneeled and crossed herself."

"We're waiting for the dark-haired woman who kneeled at Susanna's grave?"

"She doesn't remember doing it. I think she was in an altered state."

"Altered state?" What was an altered state?

A white vehicle approached, the driver waving and smiling. *Heavens above.* It was her.

"Hi," said Lisbeth. "You look great."

"Thanks. The sun works miracles."

"Of course, it can kill you, too."

"True." Linda became serious. "Lisbeth, am I alone?"

She immediately understood the nature of the question and looked directly at me. "As a matter of fact, you aren't."

She knew!

I climbed into the back seat and gazed out the window. I assumed a desert would be sandy, but natural growth abounded, and I watched a new world go by. The conversation in the front seat astounded me even more.

"So I thought we could call Ariel and ask her to help him cross over," Linda said.

"Linda, Ariel's in Florida."

"Oh no."

"Her mother's sick. She won't be back for a week."

The one I just traversed the continent to be with isn't here? Disappointment overcame me until I thought, *What is a week, when I've waited the better part of a century?*

Lisbeth dropped us off at Linda's place, a door in a series of doors in a series of look-alike buildings.

"They call these townhouses," Linda explained as we entered through a sliding door. "They're like apartments, but you own them."

Why would a person want to own part of a building and not the whole thing?

Wall-to-wall rugs covered the floors of small rooms throughout. She pulled her suitcase to the top of the staircase, then showed me to a room that belonged to her son and asked me to stay there. In addition, she asked me not to visit her when she was in bed at night.

I wouldn't want a ghost in my room at night either. But she would feel comfortable knowing I'm in the *next* room? *She must trust me,* I thought, though she didn't know me and couldn't see me. Perhaps it was because I had followed her wishes so far. At any rate, having no interest in jeopardizing this opportunity, I relaxed in the little room.

Later that evening, Linda came to the doorway. "I'm sorry," she said. "Your name isn't Edward, is it? It's Aaron."

Now, how in the world had she ascertained that blessed fact?

"I went to Lisbeth's for dinner. She channeled, and her guides told me."

I had no idea what "guides" were or how one "channeled." The fact that I would no longer be known by my father's name was enough.

"They said to tell you that when you cross, there will be plenty of time to rest. You're exhausted, aren't you?"

They knew that? What else had they told her? Then I realized something else. They said *when*, not *if*. I would have doubted this message, had she not acknowledged my true name. But given that and the fact that they knew of my exhaustion, must not the remainder be true? Was I indeed on the path to Susanna and my mother and all my loved ones?

I ruminated upon this until dawn.

❖   ❖   ❖

Linda asked me to stay at the house while she taught school. Barely aware of her departure each morning, by afternoon I'd be downstairs anticipating her return. The moment she entered she'd begin a nonstop conversation lasting well nigh into the wee hours.

She spoke aloud, said it took less effort, and sometimes I asked questions. Sometimes she even answered them.

Thursday, she came home early. "Honey, I'm home!" she called, laughing. I didn't get the joke; I was just glad to have her back.

That night, she turned on the radio, an interesting phenomenon—to be able to hear music and voices from so far away. Traveled over airwaves, she explained, same as the machine she called the "television." You could actually see pictures move on that one as if people were inside.

Tonight, we listened to a waltz. *Ah, my heartstrings.* Only once had I waltzed in life, tripping over my feet, if I recall correctly. And my partner? My bride. Painful was the recollection, more painful still when Linda asked, "Aaron, can you waltz?" She raised her arms, ready to dance. I stepped into them, and the two of us—I, the ghost, and she, the hostess—danced round the room.

How inexorable was the bond forming between us, and how strange that I no longer avoided such attachment. I needed Linda, yet did not resent my insufficiency. Neither did I wish to be alone any longer, nor did her friends or family annoy me. In fact, I found them enjoyable.

Near week's end, Linda spoke with Lisbeth on that contraption, the telephone, irritation filling her voice.

Oh no, Linda, I thought. *Don't lose patience with your loved ones. They're all you've got.*

"What do you mean?" Linda responded to Lisbeth. "I don't think so. Okay. Saturday. Bye." She slammed down the receiver and sat for a minute, then turned to me.

"I'm so sorry, Aaron. Ariel may not be back until the end of next week."

Ah, me. I went to lie down in the little room upstairs.

They still had weekends, I saw late the next morning when I found her sitting on the edge of her bed, dressing. Immediately, she covered herself with a towel. "Please don't look at me when I'm not dressed."

Embarrassed, I moved into the hall so I could not see her. But her own unease was not so much modesty as unhappiness with her appearance. She felt fat and ugly, she said, and didn't know what to do about it. She described an array of programs and remedies, none of which seemed to correct the problem. She looked okay to me. Actually, she was shaped somewhat like Maudie.

She began to cry, not only over her weight, she said, but over finances and family problems and her career. "In some ways, I'm a lot like you, Aaron. I feel so stuck." I peeked in at the same moment, as—fully dressed—she looked into the hallway. "Life isn't working, and I don't know what to do about it."

"Oh, little one," I said, "if you could only know what it really means to be stuck—to have nowhere to go, no one to talk with for decades, and be too tired to move and unable to rest on top of it. Worst of all, to be cut off from everyone you love. I hope you never have to experience this.

"But to say I am still stuck is no longer true. I have changed my way of being. No longer do I wish to be away from others. Most of all, I wish to be with my loved ones."

My loved ones. How could they possibly understand and forgive me? They had to still believe I had shirked them.

"Oh, God," I cried aloud, "I'm not the man I was. Look where I am, where I've come, what I've done. I, who once despised strangers, have followed this woman I hardly know to a place I never desired to visit because I no longer wish to be alone. Out of faith, pure faith, have I done this thing, with barely a word or whisper to go on. For the love of God, look upon this poor soul. Have mercy on me."

❖   ❖   ❖

The following week, I broke my word and accompanied Linda to school, then laid back in the car while she taught. In a flash, we were speeding down the highway. Evening it was, with everything lit up, including the panel of instruments on the dash in front of me. I attempted to determine the purpose of each when she spoke out loud just as she had that first time at her cottage, scaring the wits out of me.

"You're here!"

It hadn't occurred to me that she might sense my presence. Shocked I was, and she too, for hadn't I gone back on my word? "Ah, miss," I said, "I beg your forgiveness. It's just that it's been over a week now, and having never seen…"

"Well, as long as you're here," she said, dismissing the issue, "let me explain these instruments to you."

She had felt me studying these gadgets, though something was wrong. She addressed me as if I were in the backseat, but I sat next to her in front.

"This is the radio," she said, indicating illuminated numbers. "This is the tuner—see that red line?" Pointing with her free hand, she looked over her shoulder to the back seat.

Linda, Linda. I'm right next to you.

She gestured to the glowing gauges and explained each one. It was more than I could absorb. When she was done, she sat back. "We're almost there." I had no idea where we were going, but was

265

happy that the lesson, however intriguing, was over. "Here we are," she said, swinging into a small space between two other cars at a building that looked like Linda's but wasn't.

Where are we?

"This is Lisbeth's house." She asked me to stay in the car. Not a problem. After the driving lesson, I was all in.

"Hey! There's Liz, Ariel's daughter!"

I sat up. *Ariel's daughter?*

"Liz and Ariel live next door to Lisbeth. That's how we all know each other."

Liz and Linda hugged, then Linda asked how her grandmother was and when Ariel would return.

"Thursday," said Liz.

Only a few days!

Liz looked directly at me as I sat in the car while they talked. Then she said, "Do you know someone is in your car?" Linda hadn't spoken about me to anyone but Lisbeth. This woman could see me!

"Male or female?" Linda asked.

"Male."

"Front seat or back?"

"Front."

Linda's smile faded. "Oh." She told Liz about me. Then, "I brought him to Arizona hoping your mother could help."

A distinct pause. "Well, give her a few days."

Linda agreed, not about to push.

Ariel did return on Thursday. That evening, Linda spoke on the phone to Lisbeth, then turned to me. "Bad news. Ariel's sick."

By Saturday, Linda was more anxious than I to get the job done.

"Evan comes home tomorrow," she said to Lisbeth while they ate dinner on the patio. "I can't have a ghost in the same house as my child."

"Linda," Lisbeth said, "I don't think we need Ariel. I think we can do this ourselves."

"But, we've never done it. What if something goes wrong?"

If they had never done it before, how would they know what to do?

Linda paused, then made a decision. "Okay, it's worth a try."

They walked in from the patio and called me. I entered from the kitchen where I had been listening. They sat down, Lisbeth in the rocker by the stairs, Linda in the center of the room on a foot-stool.

"Aaron," Linda began, "We're going to help you cross over with Lisbeth's guides assisting us."

All right, I thought, *bring them on, your guides.* I looked forward to an encounter with the beings who had known my name. At the very least, perhaps they could answer a few questions.

Lisbeth closed her eyes. She inhaled deeply and exhaled noisily. For a time, she and Linda sat, silent and unmoving. Then, almost imperceptibly, Lisbeth's nose twitched, then the corner of her mouth, a spasm in her left hand. She began to speak—slowly, softly. "We are here to bring comfort and good cheer."

No longer was I alone in the Second Layer. The one who spoke—clothed in a black hooded cloak, the hair over his wrinkled forehead gray—had eyes as clear as the deep blue sea. Others stood behind him, nodding and smiling. Where had they come from?

"Oh, dear lost one," Lisbeth began, but it was no longer her voice. Her lips moved with the words, but the voice I heard was that of the old one. Then she ceased talking, and he spoke to me directly.

"You have come far in your journey, and complete it you shall, for you have found a new way of being, a way that does not separate itself from others but bonds with them as you have with this one here." He indicated Linda, who sat on the footstool beside me, her eyes closed.

As if prompted, she spoke up. "Oh! I forgot to tell Aaron goodbye!" Her voice shook with emotion, and her eyes filled as she declared, "Tell him I'll miss him." She had been my companion and friend in the truest sense. "Tell him I want to meet him when I come over."

"I'll be there waiting for you, little one. I love you," I said.

Lisbeth repeated my words.

And then, glory of glories, the ceiling opened up and disappeared as a Light greater than any I have ever seen before or since, parted the sky. This Light was for me, and in that Light stood three figures, two in front, one behind.

They had come.

Sean and Eloise stepped forward, arms open, greeting me with smiles and joy and laughter. "Oh my dears. Oh my dears." I moved into their arms and burst into tears. Little Katy ran up, laughing, so happy to see me—me, the one who had despised her wondrous love for her mother! "Oh, forgive me. Forgive me," I cried, and we wept and hugged, and kissed each other a hundred times over.

Then in a twinkling, I looked up, and there she was, waiting behind them, just as I had envisioned—beautiful, glowing, her arms outstretched. Swiftly I moved to her, enfolding her in my own arms, kissing her beautiful lips, her face, her neck. "Ah,

Susanna, my Susanna, you have come for me at last." Tears streamed over us, hers mixing with mine, forming a great river of relief and joy and gratitude.

I turned to my Eloise, my Sean, my Katy, opening my arms to include them, and we all embraced—the five of us—and cried. Out loud I cried, and so did they.

It was a grand and glorious crossing, and when I looked back, the little sitting room was no more. The hooded guide-angel raised his hand in blessing, kissing two fingers and bringing them to his forehead and out to me in a salute. Then he, too, vanished.

It was done. I was home.

AFTERWORD

Let me tell you how it felt when Aaron crossed.

First of all, Lisbeth and I had never done anything like this before. Although we'd been working spiritually by channeling with each other for years, crossing a ghost over is something we'd never even thought of trying. So when she said she thought we could do it, I was doubtful, to say the least. But Evan would be coming home the next day, and my options were running out.

When she and I work together, one of us channels by going into a meditative trance. It feels like floating. Sometimes we feel another energy flowing down over or into us. I usually feel a pleasant tingling after a while. The other supports the trance through meditation until the one channeling begins to speak, then picks up pencil and paper and takes dictation, since neither of us remembers exactly what is said during session otherwise—which makes sense, since what is said is not a product of our own mind. Instead, it just comes through and is translated by it. The concepts, although clear and sometimes accompanied by images, are not our own. Coming through from an altered state—meditation—the channeler just passes on the message. Stopping to think about it breaks the flow and can bring you out of the meditation entirely.

The idea behind channeling is that dimensions we can't see exist—where beings have access to greater wisdom than we do—and connect with us at higher levels of thought than our ordinary, everyday consciousness. Meditation takes away the mind-chatter that distracts and keeps us in that low thought level.

On this evening, I was so involved in the event that I didn't look for pencil or paper. I did support Lisbeth's trance by going into a light meditation, but stayed with what happened in the room. When her guide, Simeon, came through and she began to talk, he spoke directly to Aaron, saying, "Oh dear, lost one," and that was it. I opened my eyes. Clearly, she watched something happening behind her closed eyes, but she didn't say another word.

Then I realized I'd forgotten an important point! "Tell Aaron I said goodbye." I thought about how much fun it had been to have him with me, how exciting and unique and how honored I'd felt to be the one to bring him to this place. I didn't know if he could still hear me. "Tell him I'll miss him. I want to meet him when I cross over."

"He says he'll be there, waiting."

Well, that did it. I began to cry. Then I cried hard—to the point that I thought this was a little more than the moment called for.

Suddenly the air was clear and light. The emotion of the moment before was gone. I gasped and looked around. "He's gone!"

And then I knew. Something I couldn't see had been happening to Aaron that I must have psychically "picked up." That's why my crying felt out of place. It was their crying I picked up on. When he passed completely out of our dimension, the emotion disappeared, and I didn't feel like crying any more.

Then Simeon spoke to me through Lisbeth. "'Tis is a wondrous thing you have done," he said. "But we caution you not to go into cemeteries calling out to similar entities. Others may not be so benign and ready as this one." I thanked the guides, and it was over.

Now, you may ask why Aaron could finally cross over. First, he proved long ago—by being there for his children when they passed on—that he cared about them. Secondly, I've come to the conclusion that our journey together across the continent developed Aaron's ability to trust another. It also defined the extent of his desire to be with others. He had totally transformed from the person who avoided other people to one who could enjoy strangers from a different culture—even a different dimension!—than his. Aaron loved us. "Love you still," I hear him say as I type these words. The old Aaron wouldn't have done what he did with me.

This experience taught me so much. I'm still learning as I work on this. I don't think we're meant to know and understand everything. It would take away the fun (fun?) of going through the experience here on earth. But the veil between life and the afterlife is thin and lifts every once in a while for us to peek over to the "Other Side."

I didn't need any more proof that Aaron existed than I got that afternoon when he pressed down on my bed. The bumps the night before weren't quite like seeing that mattress go down. Those, I could still ascribe to imagination. But not the mattress.

Of course you can only take my word about what I saw. But I'm telling you, he pushed that mattress down. Whether the rest of this story is 100% accurate—it probably isn't. As the information funnels through me, my reception and translation colors it.

But what I felt at the cemetery was real. He wouldn't have followed me if I hadn't felt him enough to call out in the first place. And the emotion at his crossing, then the shock of clear space I felt after he crossed—that, I couldn't make up.

A little side note. A month ago (it's April 2005 as I write this), a part-Irish friend of mine visited her aunt, who brought out their family tree. The old woman spoke about each person as she pointed to the name. Now, my friend had read Aaron's story, so when her aunt said something about "Arön," (pronounced Ah-RONE— the "o" a combination of OH and UH), she said, "Excuse me?"

Her aunt repeated it.

My friend looked at the spelling, and said, "Aha!"

Later, she told me, "I think I know the spelling of your ghost's name."

I looked it up on the Internet, and sure enough, "Aron" is there with an umlat (double dot) over the o, a single dot over the A, meaning that the pronunciation is what I heard in my head the day I began taking Aaron's story down. I'd never heard the name pronounced that way, even though Aaron said that his father pronounced it in "the Irish way." In fact, Erin, Aaron and Aron all mean the same thing: "Ireland."

To paraphrase Aaron, life is a mystery until it is over and the sense of it is revealed. Knowing this, isn't it possible that we might not have to wait until the end to see that, in retrospect, it all will make sense? Look at the real pronunciation of Aaron's name, for example. I'd never heard anything like it before. But I trusted it. Five years later, that piece of the puzzle is solved.

Our task is to recognize that today's experiences, however chaotic or unpleasant, fit. Without knowing any more than we do now, all we have to do is trust—and live them out.

And the best part of it all?

Death is *never* the end of the story.

ACKNOWLEDGMENTS

Aaron's Crossing developed with the benefit of incredible guidance, both spiritual and from people right here on earth. Although each step in the process was a leap of faith, I never had to fly by the seat of my pants.

I have many folks to thank, beginning with all of the people who lived through this experience with me (albeit, for some, unwittingly). More than characters in a book, they are important people in my life who have shown incredible love to me and support for the project over the ten years since. They are Jan Rathburg and her son, Andrew; our friend, Carolyn Hubbard; Liz Dawn and her mom, Ariel Wolfe; my brother, Bill Dewey, his wife Carol and their daughter Sarah; my sons, Todd and Evan Bauerle; my parents; and Lisbeth Applefield.

This book developed from taking dictation in a rough narrative form without punctuation (using Aaron's real middle and last name) into a smooth manuscript with the aid of feedback from many readers. Paul Cohen, my ex-husband, read each day's installment as it came hot off the printer. Dianne Nichols, my sister, was the first person outside our house to read it.

Then it spread. First to Barb Siepker and the Writers' Collective at the Cottage Book Shop in Glen Arbor, including Kaye Bos, Joanna Pepe, and Mary Lu Fennell, my first real editor. Much appreciation to our Tuesday night book group—Jane Greiner; Jay Littel; Karen Coussens; Mary Sutherland—thanks for passing it out; Margie Herndon; Sue Woodward, my business partner and manager—for choosing *Aaron's Crossing* as one of our books to study. Dick Devinney—thanks for your stand on keeping this nonfiction when my faith flagged. Marion Devinney—you've been behind this project all the way. Nadine Weirich, thank you for your love and healing support—and our great spiritual listening group! Cheri Bieberich, Susan Steadman and Nancy Koenigbauer—that means you, too!

Thanks to all the readers in my family—Barbara Kausler, Sue and Jeff Palisin, Stacey and Tom Pezzetti! George Kausler, I appreciate your marketing efforts! More cousin-readers—Susan Johnson, Shirley McDaid, Laurie Flanigan, and Cheryl Carey. Thanks, Mom and Dad, for your editing, feedback and support.

To "Beach Readers" Sue Raymond, Gail Webster and Sally Payne—thank you! "Up North" readers with helpful feedback include Laura Murphy, Pam Hargreaves, Kathie Hicks, Sharon Scanlon, Jacki Gibler, Tina Taghon, Anne Pelham, Janet Fulton, Karen Hall, Bonnie Szydlowski, Gwen Denny, Dr. Dorian Parent—chiropractor extraordinaire, Cheri Bieberich and John Shanklin at Evolve in "downtown" Glen Arbor, Joanne Wilson, Susan Stites, and Bob Jones. There are so many to thank, I apologize if I've left you out!

Mollie and George Weeks, thanks for your efforts. Leonard Overmyer, author of *The Forest Haven Soldiers: the Civil War Veterans of Sleeping Bear and Surrounding Leelanau,* thanks for confirming that "there are some Irish" civilians buried at the Forest Haven Cemetery. Evidently, the records have disappeared, so you're the expert. Thanks to Aunt Sue, "Auntie Kleave," Carolyn Ballou, Jeff Thompson, Jim Nichols, Bob Fingers, Aaron Elson, Liz Bruening and Pete Zeutendyk for the great moral support.

Over the past five years, many lifelong friends helped with editing and feedback. Norine Stewart, who learned how to "listen" from reading *Aaron's Crossing*; Sue McGuire; Sarah Gehrke; Barb Globensky; and my first career mentor and terrific school principal, Mary Heimbecker Birchman. More dear friends to thank for reading—Jim Chaput, Gail Ash, and Erie Nagle.

Arizona friends to whom I attribute much are led by rebbe Michael Shapiro; Ruth Mower; Marsha Mower, Marion Esther, and everyone at Vision Quest in Scottsdale. To those at the Higher Self in Traverse City, Michigan, and everyone, again, at Evolve in Glen Arbor, thank you for being there for me.

So many people in my daily life have taken an interest in *Aaron's Crossing,* I can't list them all, but here are a few: Mark and everyone at the Huntington Bank in Empire, Mary and everyone at The Knit Shoppe, Dr. Van Draght's office, Marion and Vickie at Doc Houghton's, Linda at the Glen Arbor Athletic Club and all my friends there, my friends at the EUMC church; and finally, Deena and Dana, Tom and Shannon, Gregg, Nancy, Kelly, Mary, Diane, Stephanie, Kevin and Rhondi at Studio Josef's—that place rocks!

Speaking of rockin, let's not forget my music friends who played (no pun) such an important part in bringing me out of my shell. Bob Stevenson, Bobby Jones and Freddie G on the drums, how great was jammin with you guys? Brother Bill, thanks for hooking me up with them. Freddie and Bob Stevenson, thanks for getting me to the Cedar Tavern on Wednesday nights, where I found even more new friends. Deb Marois, thank you for sharing your intuition. Mike, Murph, Tim, and Joe of the great Stray Dogs and their counterpart The Fabulous Horndogs—thanks for letting me get up with you guys every once in a while to sing with you and play a few tunes. To my buddies from New Third/Two-Thirds Coast—Chris, John, and Patrick— the only way to fly on Friday nights was at the WAG with you.

To all the supporters on the Henry Ford High School Forum at DelphiForums.com including Diana Fahey, Victoria Ewald, Nancy, Miriam, Janet, the Mary's, Fran, Jean, Teri, Barb, Ruth, Deb, Donna and author Bob Bailey—thank you!

Getting into the book business has taken the research equivalent of a college education in writing, marketing and publishing. I attribute any success I have to the following educators in my life: New York agent Jim Cypher, who early on taught me that the difference between "wannabe's" and "gonnabe's" is persistence; Jen Glatzer and all the contributors at AbsoluteWrite.com. Aimé Merizon of Marinus Press, thank you for the final edit, typesetting and getting this to the printer. And thank you for that message on my answering machine right after you first read the manuscript four years ago, confirming what an amazing work this is. That one phone message carried me for a long time. Ashlea Jane Walter of Third Coast Design, thanks for getting us started.

Tom Carr and the *Traverse City Record-Eagle*, Cymbre Foster and Amy Hubbell at the *Leelanau Enterprise*, your articles began a new phase of "The Aaron Project." Chris Carlson at Horizon Books, thank you for believing in *Aaron's Crossing* and giving it exposure by hosting the play based on the book—before the book even came out! To everyone participating in the show, *Aaron's Crossing*, thank you for creating such magic: Norm Wheeler, Tina

Taghon, Duane Campbell, Laura Murphy, Alan Ladomer, Evan Bauerle, Debbie Conner, Bill Dungjen and Phil Cuchetti.

Sue Woodward—my business partner, friend, and support system—who would have thought when we were in high school together that we would end up doing this?!! You are a great manager, always thinking outside the box. Bless you for believing in me.

And finally, I want to express great appreciation to my son, Todd Bauerle for the cover design, the great website and for being the wonderful man he is; to his wife, Jenafer, for her continued valuable support and friendship; and to my younger son, Evan Bauerle, for putting up with the artist in me.

To Aaron, his family and friends and to my helpers on the Other Side—bless you all for this wondrous work.

About the Author

Linda Alice Dewey was born into a family with a metaphysical belief system that did not include ghosts. In 1987, she began exploring New Age metaphysics, commencing a fresh spiritual journey. She developed spiritual skills which include high spiritual listening, automatic writing, psychometry, mediumship, face readings and general readings.

An award-winning writer and composer in school, Dewey later taught music, art and remedial reading for nearly twenty years. In the 1980's, she wrote and produced music jingles for radio and television in Michigan and Arizona. No stranger to the stage, she's been in musical and theatrical productions all her life. A versatile singer, she continues to perform music that varies from classical (as a legitimate mezzo-soprano) to rock and blues.

Dewey co-facilitates a spiritual listening group in Glen Arbor and teaches metaphysical workshops. She resides just a mile from the wooded cemetery where she first encountered Aaron Burke. Her current projects include adapting *Aaron's Crossing* to the stage in a *Phantom*-like musical with original music. She has two grown sons and a daughter-in-law. *Aaron's Crossing* is her first book.